MW01680999

FREEDOM OF CHOICE, NO FREEDOM OF CONSEQUENCES

Developing Social Skills for Young Adults Through Critical Thinking

PART 3
NAVIGATING CHALLENGES WITH RESILIENCE

By
Dr. Douglas Allan Portello

Navigating Challenges with Resilience

FREEDOM OF CHOICE, NO FREEDOM OF CONSEQUENCES

By

Dr. Douglas Allan Portello

ISBN (E-Book): 978-1-966167-39-6
ISBN (Paperback): 978-1-966167-40-2

This Book is Meant to...

This book guides you to become more aware of your thoughts and actions by using reflection and critical thinking. It highlights how every event, big or small, shapes your future. Every decision leads to new choices, underscoring the importance of wise decision-making. By sharing my journey as a young adult, this book seeks to inspire you to reflect on your decisions to foster personal growth, success, and fulfillment.

Self-reflection and critical thought are not just tools; they are the foundation of your decision-making journey. They are the keys needed to unlock a better version of yourself. Without their full development, your life may not be what you truly desire but a reflection of others' lower expectations. Living without self-reflection and critical thinking will lead to a less fulfilling life, especially when surrounded by others who do not engage in these practices either.

Decisions made without self-reflection and critical thinking will yield significantly different outcomes and have a profoundly different impact on your life than those made with these principles in mind. Consequently, decisions formed in self-reflection provide you with a more direct path to achieving your goals. Remember that you are the architect of your life, and it's important to consider how you want your life to unfold. As the architect, you must think critically about your decisions, seek advice from others, and remain open to change. By doing so, you stay in control of your life and create meaningful progress.

The quality of your decisions directly impacts the movement and outcomes you experience. While this may not always be immediately apparent, a careful assessment reveals that it is true. Decisions based on sound, critical thinking can make the difference between an average life and a great one. For instance, critical thinking can open doors that lead to better opportunities, such as selecting the most effective academic path or the most suitable career route. It can also improve your relationships by helping you understand others' perspectives. Furthermore, it's important to be critical of the company (friends, acquaintances, etc.) you keep, as they can significantly influence your decisions. The company you keep will either produce a positive force, helping you cultivate better decision-making skills, or form a barrier to your progression.

The advice in this book may sound repetitive compared to what you have already heard. What is written here is nothing you have yet to hear before in some fashion. Although the ideas and concepts presented in this book may not be revolutionary, I aimed to make them relevant to young adults. These are the crucial years for personal development and life-changing decision-making. I want the concepts in this book to resonate with you when you are ready to think about them meaningfully. Therefore, if the ideas and concepts resonate with you, reflect on their broader meaning.

If the guidance in this book doesn't resonate with you the first time you read it, consider holding on to it and revisiting it later, perhaps a year or two. By 'holding on to the book,' I mean keeping it in a place where you can easily find it. Doing so lets you revisit specific chapters when their concepts become more relevant to your lived experiences. As a result, the guidance in this book will resonate with you on a more personal level.

While it's true this book may not reach everyone who could benefit from it, the potential impact is significant for those who do. This book provides scaffolding through a narrative to support better decision-making. Your potential for growth as a young adult is immense, and I hope this book fills you with hope and optimism for your journey. It is essential to understand that an accurate measure of learning is its practical application. Thus, you can demonstrate your growth by applying the knowledge to understand the concepts, then applying them to your life to gain wisdom.

Life's journey often involves trial and error, leading to frustration and disappointment. As a result, navigating life can be challenging, especially for those who lack someone to support them or a resource to help them improve their situation. With this understanding, I aimed to ease those challenges. This book is designed to help reduce disappointment during these exploratory phases by sharing insights and wisdom gained from years of experience.

Living by trial and error is a natural part of life, but it's not the only way to learn, nor is it the most productive. What is productive is listening and learning from others who have made mistakes. Their experiences can provide a better path with the fewest errors and setbacks. This book can guide you, providing insights and strategies to help you make more informed decisions and navigate life's challenges with greater confidence and resilience. Remember, you're not alone in this journey.

This book offers benefits in two significant ways. First, it provides tangible value through a collection of inspiring quotes, and second, it imparts intangible life lessons. The tangible value is clear: each chapter begins with a quote. Memorizing these quotes can help establish a framework for your life in areas you want to improve. They can also boost your motivation and continually inspire you. Quotes are concise reflections of the wisdom gleaned from others' experiences. Therefore, you are encouraged to memorize a few quotes that resonate with you, as they encapsulate valuable insights succinctly.

The intangible value, however, is more complex. It consists of two essential components: 'given' and 'acceptance.' This book provides the 'given'—a message that underscores the importance of critical thinking. Therefore, the 'given' is discovered through the words of the book as one reads it, uncovering its meaningful concepts and advice. On the other hand, the 'acceptance' is something you must consciously develop and embrace on your own. Therefore, the 'acceptance' is earned through a willingness to integrate this advice into your decision-making process.

In this context, 'acceptance' means acknowledging the importance of critical thinking in decision-making and being open to applying it in your life. It's about recognizing that critical thinking is a skill and a mindset that can bring positive change. Hearing counsel or reading advice is only half the battle toward being healthier; the other half is implementing the knowledge into understanding. Hence, your actions develop your thinking to change your life.

Why is this book geared toward young adults? This is the age range where resources are available to make life-changing decisions. It is the interim between middle school (learning who you are) and adulthood (visualizing who you want to be). The young adult phase is a time to make informed decisions and lay the groundwork for a solid future as a mature adult. A mature adult does not resemble the atmosphere of a person's middle or high school years. Adult life is more brutal and unforgiving than either of these places. As an adult, there is often no opportunity to revisit events to improve or correct them, as a young person can usually do during their intermediate and secondary schooling years.

For instance, middle school grades are not the determining factor for moving into high school. A student passes through middle school based on age, even if all course grades are F's. A high school student can also put in minimal effort and pass through their high school years based on age. However, as an adult, everything has significance. In adulthood, reaching the next meaningful milestone requires effort. There are no free passes to reach the next meaningful milestone without the necessary effort. As an adult, you either strive to do things well, use your experiences to build a better life, or remain stuck in the same routine until you find the motivation to change. Hence, forming sound decision-making skills is vital.

Employers often view young adults who excel academically as likely to bring the same level of effort and thoughtfulness to their work. Their ability to develop critical thinking skills strongly indicates how they will navigate their careers. Furthermore, employers are less interested in young adults who do not demonstrate effort or enthusiasm for learning or managing their lives. After all, why would employers be interested in or hire someone who lacks a commitment to achieve in education or improve their decision-making? They won't?

The following is a short example of what this book offers. As a former teacher and substitute for over a decade, I've seen firsthand how often students rush through their thinking without pausing to reflect before acting. In their minds, they want what they want, and before they realize it, their choices have set them on a path shaped by actions that can't easily be undone—or by patterns that may prove harmful over time. In their mind, for example, if students ask to use the bathroom, they sign out of class and take a designated 'hall pass' used for this purpose. Leaving the classroom for this type of event should take a few minutes, and the student should return to class promptly.

The problem is that some students do not return to the classroom for 15 minutes, and sometimes even 20. The assumption is they met up with friends from another classroom (after texting one another beforehand). Another possibility is the student spent the time with someone during a different lunch period. This is the kind of decision-making example commonly found among young adults. Their freedom of choice is always there, but poor decision-making can have life-changing consequences.

Students who develop and practice decision-making geared toward deception and evasion cultivate poor habits. These behaviors are harmful, as they often become stronger with repetition. Patterns of deceit can last a lifetime; therefore, young adults who have established these tendencies are more likely to continue deceiving others, motivated by past successes in evading accountability. Hence, this book is essential for understanding, addressing, and making necessary corrections as a young adult.

This book enables young adults to examine and reflect on their actions from various relatable perspectives, helping them modify their decision-making habits. While applying the book's insights and reflecting on its stories may be challenging, it's worth remembering that they represent real experiences young adults encounter in life.

Lastly, this book also provides 'critical thinking' narrative sections between every couple of chapters. These sections foster a reflective dialogue with readers, highlighting how life can improve when focused on a specific attribute. Each critical thinking section highlights one personal quality, such as self-awareness, discipline, accountability, stewardship, etc. Reading these sections allows the reader to reflect on the meaning of the attributes and assimilate them into their life.

Table Of Contents

PART 3
NAVIGATING CHALLENGES WITH RESILIENCE

Conducting early investigations, such as seeking feedback on projects before they are due and addressing misunderstandings with colleagues as soon as they arise, are valuable strategies that can help you avoid frustration. Addressing problems promptly can prevent them from escalating into significant challenges. This is because issues often worsen over time, so it is crucial to tackle them early. Don't be afraid to explore the unknown; doing so will help achieve a quick resolution and save resources.

Being proactive and addressing issues early can prevent future frustration and better prepare you for what lies ahead. The key here is not to let problems fester but to confront them directly, regardless of their unknowns. A benefit of early investigation is that it can significantly enhance problem-solving skills and contribute to personal development.

Life has a way of creeping up on us and gradually slowing us down, reminding us of our mortality and the limits of our time. This realization can sometimes trap us in the mentality that life is plentiful and that we can maintain the same pace we once did, even when we make unhealthy choices or neglect other important areas. Unfortunately, that's not the reality we face. To break free from this illusion, we need guidance. One valuable source of support is mentors. They can take your skills from good to great, helping you navigate life's challenges.

While on your journey of success, stay calm and look for ways to navigate adverse events. For instance, in a job interview, staying calm can help you answer questions more effectively and make a good impression. Similarly, in a heated argument, staying calm can help you respond more thoughtfully and avoid saying something you might regret. Remaining calm in difficult times can be developed through dedication, patience, and consistent practice.

Speaking of practice, the ten-thousand-hour rule is generally accepted as the time required to master a skill and achieve a high level of competence. The concept holds that putting in 10,000 hours of progressive practice will achieve mastery at the highest level. The rule is not restricted to any specific area of life but can serve as a guide, showing that with time, effort, and perseverance, you can accomplish anything exceptionally well. Understanding this concept can be a powerful motivator, inspiring you to strive for mastery in your chosen field.

In essence, it's ultimately up to you how you choose to spend your time. Know that minor disruptions become less significant once you establish a consistent routine in activities you find valuable. When balancing items in your life that matter to you, remember that setbacks are a natural part of any journey. It's important to take responsibility for your feelings about your inconveniences rather than blaming others or external circumstances. Taking on this personal responsibility empowers you to take charge of your journey.

Chapter 1
Do not be Afraid to Investigate

Curiosity will conquer fear even more than bravery will.

— **James Stephens**

Twenty years from now you will be more disappointed by the things that you didn't do than by the ones you did do. So, throw off the bowlines. Sail away from the safe harbor. Catch the trade winds in your sails. Explore. Dream. Discover.

— **Mark Twain**

Conducting early investigations is a valuable strategy that can help you avoid frustration. For example, don't hesitate to investigate an issue if you notice a discrepancy on a work project or have a misunderstanding in a course assignment. Addressing problems promptly can prevent them from escalating into significant challenges. Issues often worsen over time, so it is crucial to tackle them early. Know that staying calm during tough times is a skill that can be cultivated with commitment, patience, and regular practice.

Being proactive and addressing issues early can prevent future frustration and better prepare you for what lies ahead. These unknown factors can range from a lack of communication with colleagues to project mix-ups.

However, the key is not to let these problems fester but to confront them directly. By addressing issues promptly, you can better understand the situation and access the necessary resources and coping strategies. Early intervention not only reduces anxiety but also fosters a sense of security, helping you develop resilience and adaptive skills, ultimately contributing to improved mental well-being and a greater likelihood of long-term positive outcomes.

Furthermore, engaging in early investigation is a practice that can significantly enhance your problem-solving skills and contribute to your personal development. Investigating the unknown can be scary sometimes; I get that. However, during early investigations, you will realize that some issues are better than you anticipated, and you will be glad you investigated them. Remember, the more you investigate, the more invested you become and the more hopeful you can be about the potential positive outcomes. For instance, noticing a discrepancy in a project at work can prevent a significant error that might have cost valuable time and resources.

It opens your mind, reduces fear, and makes you more receptive to learning. Do not allow fear to stop you from investigating. Channeling fear into your curiosity is beneficial and essential for investigating unknown issues. This mindset of lowering your fear threshold and allowing it to lead to curiosity can yield more positive outcomes and a more open, engaged approach to problem-solving. Keep in mind that early investigation prevents potential problems and builds confidence in problem-solving skills, making you better prepared for future challenges. Embrace the fear of the unknown and the humility that comes from not knowing what lies ahead, and let it evolve into a sense of curiosity.

Investing your time to investigate a problem or concern can be quite beneficial, and it doesn't have to take much time. Sometimes, it can be as simple as asking for clarification or taking a slight detour in your approach to explore a better option or resource. For example, seeking clarification on work projects or school assignments can save you time when there isn't much available. If you're unsure about an issue or have a concern, take the initiative to investigate. Clearing away doubts and misunderstandings will provide you with a more straightforward path.

If you feel disappointed you don't know something someone else does, ask a question, learn about it, and then you will know. Remember, the other person who does know also had to learn the information from somewhere. They must have asked questions to someone who knew the answer. There was a time when they did not know. Hence, it is okay that you do not know. But once you ask questions, you will begin to know. Don't be afraid to investigate. Asking questions is a powerful tool that puts you in control of your learning. It's not just about finding the answer; it's about curiosity and engaging in learning.

Suppose you made your first inquiry but are still awaiting the answer you sought. This is a significant step because you've already set the wheels in motion to find a solution, which was likely the most challenging part. The fear of being exposed as a person who does not know is now behind you. Consequently, the initial resistance you felt before asking the question has dissipated. You're now experiencing a lower level of anxiety and can continue to ask until you find what you're looking for. I urge you to embrace curiosity and seek answers rather than hold back.

Let me share an example in my life. I was assembling an academic project that required approval at several levels before finalization. Each time I turned in a section, I waited for feedback. The anticipation was nerve-wracking. After making changes based on the feedback, I would resubmit my corrected project and wait for further feedback. Having the project in their queue was a combination of mixed feelings for me. On one hand, it was a relief because it was off my 'to-do' list. Conversely, it also caused me stress, as I felt anxious about when I would get it back—along with comments—or what those comments might entail.

Over the next several months, the anxiety and stress about waiting for comments became so heightened that I did not want to open my email inbox for fear of seeing their response to my project. Basically, I was afraid to investigate. I did not want to be exposed to the unknown. It was a terrible feeling to be held emotionally captive by the possibility of receiving an email from them. I considered the days without their response to be good days because my project would still be in their queue.

Before this entire project began (a couple of years ago), I checked my email daily, sometimes twice a day. I did not mind receiving emails from anyone about anything. However, after the project was underway, I dreaded opening my inbox so much that I only opened it once a week. This fear and avoidance had a tangible impact on my project. I had nothing personal against the person correcting my work; it was the feeling of the unknown issues I would need to fix when I received an email about my work that caused the anxiety. I was not a fan of the uncertainties surrounding unresolved issues. Avoiding this fear of the unknown prompted me to be more assertive in my investigation.

I confronted my fear of receiving emails about my project by telling myself that the situation would not improve if I let them sit in my inbox. Basically, not opening my inbox to avoid the anxiety was not going to help matters. Any email I received from them was not going to disappear because I didn't want to open it. Therefore, I might as well open it, address the required feedback, and send the project back as soon as possible. I committed to returning to the daily routine of checking my email and tackling whatever messages came in that day. Whether an email was from them or not, I addressed any issue that day.

Through this new investigative process, I adopted a more active role in addressing unknown events, shifting from a reactive to a proactive stance. As a result, this proactive approach has alleviated my fears of uncertainty, helping me manage otherwise distressing situations more effectively.

While I have moved on from that project, it did delay my completion date and cost me thousands of dollars in lost time. It also required extending the deadline, for which I needed to put out additional resources to compensate for the delay. It was an expensive lesson in being afraid of the unknown and developing a sense of anxiety, which became detrimental to my progression.

I urge you to take a proactive role in your life's events. It's a transformative approach that can make a significant difference in how you feel about the unknown. To overcome your fear of investigating the unknown, try setting a specific time each day for investigation, or start with smaller, less intimidating unknowns and work your way up to issues that carry the weight of being significant. Remember, the more you investigate, the more hopeful you can be about the potential positive outcomes. This empowerment will make you feel more confident and in control of the unknowns that hold you captive from advancing.

Taking a different view on fear, people seldom feel fear when doing familiar things. A couple of reasons for this are that familiar situations are associated with lower levels of anxiety compared to unknown situations. Another is that a person's confidence is higher in familiar situations. The emotions a person feels about an action depend primarily on their expectations of its outcome. Therefore, investigating familiar problems is more frequent and less anxiety-provoking than investigating unfamiliar situations. Investigating the unknown can be discomforting, whereas familiarity provides comfort and confidence, making a person feel more secure and at ease.

Therefore, let me encourage you to familiarize yourself with 'investigating the unknown.' This means that even though 'new' situations (unknown) may be unfamiliar, as any new situation tends to be, you would be better served considering them as familiar. Consider them to be familiar in the sense all 'new' situations have their specific category of being 'new' and that you are familiar with 'new' being troublesome.

Hence, instead of viewing 'new' situations as reasons to shy away, consider them like the rest of the world: unfamiliar until you investigate. In this way, all unfamiliar situations can shift from high anxiety about the unknown problem to low anxiety of being categorized as traditionally unfamiliar situations, which you have been exposed to many times.

The key point in this mental shift is to let the 'results' of your investigation be the unknown, not the initial situation. Telling yourself the initial situation is unknown will stop you from wanting to investigate. If you let the 'results' of your curiosity remain unknown, you are more likely to start investigating unfamiliar situations, which is good. Therefore, do not let the idea of the initial investigation be the unknown; let the result after you have started investigating be the unknown.

Remember, the fear of the unknown is a natural part of living life, and by embracing it, you open yourself up to new possibilities and growth. Therefore, embrace the unknown and be curious when you are given the opportunity. You'll soon realize that 'unknowns' are not something to fear but a gateway to personal development and problem-solving, offering you the chance to learn and grow in ways you never thought possible.

When responding to an unfamiliar situation, it is natural to feel uncertain about the outcome. However, in some cases, the conclusions of investigations will be positive and exceed your expectations. This is because it is unlikely to tell whether the result of any unknown will positively or negatively affect you until an answer or resolution is found. Furthermore, it is difficult to determine, with any certainty, whether a result will have a costly or inexpensive resolution until you find the answer. However, a prompt investigation often leads to a less expensive outcome.

The act of investigation is not the potential problem but an opportunity to be proactive and embrace new possibilities. Therefore, don't be afraid to explore. Remember, only the initial perception of the unknown outcome makes delving into the unknown difficult. The fear of the unknown is a natural part of the process, and by embracing it, you open yourself up to new possibilities and personal growth. Investigating the unknown can also build confidence and adaptability as you navigate unfamiliar situations.

It makes sense that people dive deeper into personal matters when things change from consistent to inconsistent. From my experience, people feel compelled to engage in self-reflection and situational analysis when things have gone wrong. In contrast, engaging in this investigative process is unnecessary when things are going well.

For example, if your vehicle sounds and operates fine, there is no need to investigate. If you excel in your academic education and get good grades, there is no real need to engage in discussions with faculty or other students to improve. If there are no arguments or disappointments between you and your friends, and your relationships with others are okay, there is no real need to investigate to improve them. Why would you need to engage in self-reflection if nothing you notice is wrong in your life? There is no need to, right?

It's important to remember that self-awareness is not just a tool for fixing what's wrong but also for understanding what's right and how to maintain it. The potential for improvement with the unknowns of your life is vast, and it takes significant courage to explore them. Embracing the idea that change can lead to personal growth and development is critical. This emphasis on change should encourage you and instill a sense of determination to take that step to investigate.

It's important to remember that change requires time and energy and might throw your daily routine off course a bit. However, the advantages of exploring and implementing positive changes far outweigh the temporary disruptions to your usual schedule. Embracing this process can lead to greater long-term benefits.

Realizing that effort is required to improve one's situation is a significant step. The fear of additional work often hampers personal growth. However, by asking questions and investigating problems, you are taking control of your growth and development. This realization should boost your confidence and make you feel more in control of your journey. One of the major underlying themes of this conversation regarding proactive investigation is understanding that you are the driver of your personal growth through the questions you ask.

Better life situations and more solid foundations come at a cost. It may be unpleasant to tally the cost of improvement, but it's worth it. If you want a better life, you must be okay with some disappointment when you allocate your time and effort to improve it. Realizing this concept of balancing time for results means knowing that your free time will be spent solving issues, such as finalizing a work project, achieving better grades, or building stronger relationships.

Understanding and accepting these sacrifices of your time for self-improvement is crucial. Sacrificing your time for other things will prepare you for the journey ahead and put you in control of your growth. For instance, investigating a potential issue in a school or work project can lead to a more efficient and successful outcome, boosting your confidence and control over matters in your life. However, there is some good news about this sacrifice as you become more aligned with your ambitions and more aware of how valuable your time is.

Being mentally aligned with the resources you have (time and effort) makes you a stronger, more competent worker. It's important to take pride in evaluating the advantages of the gap between your current position and where you might be after investing your time and effort. The cost of making things better is sometimes seen as fear because you are losing in one area of your life (time and effort) for an unknown quantity somewhere else. This fear of investigation stems from three sources: ego, bodily injury, and material harm or loss.

These reasons seem rather large at first, but they are easy to explain with examples. Let us start with ego. The fear of investigating related to the ego is linked to pride. In this context, ego refers to a person's sense of self-importance or self-worth. Therefore, people don't want to know what they don't know. They don't want to be held accountable or have to put their ego in check after they become aware.

For example, consider a situation in which a team member is aware of a potential issue with a work project but chooses not to investigate it out of fear of being perceived as incompetent. This is a precise instance where ego interferes with the investigation process. In this scenario, it would be easier to ignore the problem until someone else notices it and takes the lead. Our ego is the primary factor contributing to the lack of investigation. Set aside your ego; it will save you time and effort in the long run.

Curiosity and humility go hand in hand. To be curious about the world and willing to investigate, a person must be humble, not prideful, or arrogant. Embracing humility is a journey of personal growth that leads to proper understanding. It's in a person's best interest to put aside their pride and ego about what they believe is right or what they think is going on and to be humble enough to take the time to explore the situation.

Curiosity is about setting aside our pride and ego and being open to not having all the answers. This is a challenging task, but the rewards are immense. Being humble does not come easy, nor does putting an ego on a shelf. Consequently, being humbled often leads to putting the ego on the shelf, where it belongs, to embrace the unknown. My advice for you is to put your ego on the 'shelf' before you are asked to or shown to. Keeping the ego in check will keep your fear in check and allow you to be more open about what you don't know.

Let's explore the second reason behind our fear of investigation: the risk of bodily injury. It's completely understandable to be apprehensive about physical harm when considering an investigation. After all, no one wants to place themselves in jeopardy. While it's great to be curious, there are limits, and the possibility of personal injury is undoubtedly one of them. For example, if you're investigating a potential safety concern in a project, it's crucial to weigh the risks and take the necessary precautions to protect yourself.

There will be some fear when sizing up a problem to investigate. The issue here is how to size it up. What resources are available to you? How comfortable are you with those resources? And how intensely is the problem related to your life and current situation? Regardless of our background or circumstances, we must ask ourselves these questions when considering an investigation involving bodily injury.

Imagine a situation involving self-care. You are driving your vehicle when it starts making an annoying sound. What do you do? Do you ignore it, convince yourself it's unimportant, or stop to investigate? Your decision would depend on your resources and the situation at hand. The fear factor, which can override the potential to explore, is influenced by the time of day, your location, and other variables. Ideally, avoid pulling over in a secluded area; instead, aim for the nearest well-lit service station. Therefore, if you decide to keep driving, it may be best to investigate the noise further when you feel safer.

Consider a situation in your home. In the middle of the night, you hear breaking glass and unfamiliar footsteps walking around. You would want to investigate immediately, but you would also be hesitant because it might lead to a confrontation and bodily harm. Therefore, if you need to find a safe place to hide and call law enforcement, take that route. However, this does show that bodily harm is a criterion for the fear of investigation.

Let's explore the third reason behind our fear of investigation: the potential for material harm or loss. In this context, material harm and loss refer to damage or depletion of resources. From a humanistic standpoint, it's understandable to shy away from looking into potential issues; after all, no one wants to spend money on repairs that might not be necessary or invest time in matters they don't care about. However, the downside of this avoidance is that ignoring problems only adds to our already packed schedules and increases our stress levels. As a result, we often overlook issues that should be addressed, just to sidestep confronting what truly needs our attention. It's a tough spot, but remember, you're not alone in feeling this way.

Many people overlook vehicle problems by failing to recognize the importance of regular oil changes. They often do this because they want to avoid the expense (loss to their checking account) or because they feel it will take time away from their already busy schedules (material harm). Similarly, students often miss the opportunity to review incorrect answers on homework, quizzes, and tests. They do this to save time for other activities and because they prefer to move on and forget about their mistakes. They do not want to go over wrong answers because it takes time and effort. Therefore, they view their time and energy as wasted if they have to review their mistakes.

Do you see how viewing lost time and effort as fuel that keeps the fear of investigation alive? Fear becomes the guiding principle for not acting because it will result in a loss of time or energy. In their view, finding the correct answers to missed problems will absorb their time and energy and not benefit them in the short term. They fear losing that specific amount of time and effort they could put toward doing something else -something more exciting than reviewing missed problems. However, those overlooked questions may resurface in future quizzes, tests, or even the final exam, resulting in lower grades and a lack of comprehension. This will make matters worse for them, which they cannot see through their fear.

In conclusion, facing unprepared challenges and investigating unknown situations may be daunting. However, it's crucial to understand that investigation is not something to fear. Furthermore, fear of the unknown will limit your horizons. Therefore, embrace investigating the unknown more frequently, and you'll find it easier each time. Continuously ask questions and explore the subjects you engage with. Remember, curiosity should not be seen as a time-absorbing inconvenience but as a tool that liberates you from the fear of the unknown and empowers you to take control of your life.

Chapter 2
Make Preventative Maintenance Required

If you don't schedule regular maintenance for the things that need it, they'll break down and schedule you—at the worst, most inconvenient moment.

— **Douglas Allan Portello**

Have you ever taken something for granted, only to have it fall apart or fail, leaving you in a problematic and distressing situation? Knowing how difficult situations can be, this unforeseen circumstance may have caused you pain, anxiety, or extreme discomfort because you were caught off guard. Preventive maintenance can prevent many difficult events from worsening and prevent distressful situations from escalating.

Consider this example: you're on a road trip in your car, exploring a different city or state, when suddenly, your car tire blows out. You are forced to steer the vehicle sharply to the side of the road. After stopping the car, you inspect the damage and see that one of the bald tires is flat. The nail found in the tire is not significant, and it would have only caused a small leak if the tire had decent tread. However, the tire tread was low, and instead of causing a slow leak, the tire could not withstand the pressure change and blew. The hardship of this event, being stranded on the side of the road with a flat tire, could have been entirely preventable with proactive maintenance.

When you finally get help, the car is in the tire shop, and you are in a position to think. You begin to analyze the problem and realize this situation did not have to happen the way it did. You put yourself in this situation by ignoring the signs of balding tires and failing to schedule an appointment to get new ones. Since you did not plan a time to address matters at your convenience, your vehicle is scheduling you. Now, you are forced to address the issue, no matter how inconvenient.

Imagine if the situation had been even worse: a tire could have blown out while driving on a fast-moving highway curve, causing the car to roll and flip. Thankfully, that wasn't the case. Your injury, as well as the injuries to others, could have been severe. Instead, you managed to steer the car safely to the side of the road and call for help. It's important to remember that not all unexpected events have such positive outcomes when preventative maintenance is neglected.

Picture this: you're heading to work for an important meeting or rushing to handle a last-minute family emergency. Then your vehicle tire blows out from the same small nail. While the issue can be fixed, and you could get back on the road, this is not the best time for complications. If you have a spare tire, you might tackle the problem yourself, but that will take time, and you'll miss that critical meeting or handle the urgent family matter.

Suppose you do not have a spare. You might call someone for help, such as AAA (Triple A) or a friend. AAA service can take several hours, depending on their current workload, which is not ideal if you have to sit and wait for a while. While your friend may be able to arrive sooner, it will still be inconvenient for them to go out of their way to assist you. Additionally, you'll need to purchase new tires, which could have prevented this situation from occurring in the first place.

Preventive maintenance is essential in every area of life because your time and energy are valuable. Equipment failure due to lack of maintenance can lead to unnecessary delays and strand you in high-stress situations. Neither of these situations do you want to be in. By incorporating necessary preventative maintenance into your daily schedule now and then, you can address issues promptly and reduce costs, as you'll manage them on your terms.

Addressing tire issues can be expensive when a tire blows, as it requires time to purchase and wait for installation. However, a significant benefit of preventative maintenance is addressing the problem at a time that works for you, saving you from more expensive repairs later. Most importantly, by addressing potential issues in advance, you avoid the stress and inconvenience of waiting for assistance on someone else's schedule.

By being prepared and proactive in your life, you can enjoy the peace of mind that comes from not being caught off guard. This is the power of proactive maintenance—it saves you from immediate inconvenience and sets you up for a smoother, less stressful future. In the long run, the time, effort, and money you save by avoiding potential accidents, breakdowns, failures, and added fees far outweigh the initial inconvenience of proactive upfront maintenance.

On the other hand, if you keep putting things off and allow potential issues to fester, your chances of success are about as slim as hitting the jackpot in the lottery. Imagine this scenario: your tire blows out while driving at night, and no tire repair shops are open, or you're stranded on a long stretch of highway without a service or towing station in the area. In these situations, fixing your tire will take much longer and cost you more. To make matters worse, if a tire shop doesn't have your budget-friendly tire in stock, you will need to spend more on a pricier alternative.

What if the nearest 'mom and pop' tire shop you are towed to doesn't carry your tire brand in your size? Then, you could be stuck in an unfamiliar town, waiting for the next shipment of tires. Adverse events could keep piling up against you if you ignore preventative maintenance and the right storm hits at the worst time. However, by taking care of scheduled preventive maintenance before it takes over your life, you can sit back in the peace of mind that comes with knowing you're prepared for most unforeseen situations.

The prior examples were simple flat tires due to the lack of vehicle preventative maintenance. In these cases, you might be inconvenienced by the need to repair the tire yourself or tow it to a shop. However, these examples don't consider the more serious consequences, such as causing an accident due to a blown tire or damaging your vehicle by losing control. In such events, you may also receive a citation or ticket if you caused an accident or hit an object owned by the county. According to Cars.com (2024), the average cost of a car accident resulting from poor maintenance is between $2,500 and $5,000. In contrast, regular maintenance costs are significantly lower, making it a financially wise choice.

One thing is sure: across all the possible aspects of an event, given your time, effort, and stress, it will be advantageous to engage in preventive maintenance at your convenience. Take care of issues related to your life (vehicle, home, friendships, work, etc.) on your own time, and do not allow them to catch you by surprise, making the situation more serious than it needs to be. You can avoid these stressful situations by taking the initiative and scheduling maintenance on your terms. Don't wait for things to schedule you; take control and prioritize your proactive maintenance.

To move away from the concept of vehicle maintenance and write in more general terms, interchange the word 'maintenance' with anything in your life that needs attention. Maintenance is simply the act of maintaining, protecting, defending, guarding, and preserving someone or something. Remember, whether it's your car, your health, or your relationships, proactive maintenance is the key to a smoother, less stressful future. Regular exercise and healthy eating can prevent health issues, just as open communication and quality time can strengthen relationships.

Regular health check-ups, spending quality time with loved ones, maintaining a healthy work-life balance, and even setting aside time for self-care are forms of proactive maintenance across different parts of life. Brushing your teeth every day is an example of preventative maintenance. If done correctly and adequately, it prevents costly dentist bills and long hours sitting in a dentist's chair. If you brush and floss after each meal, or at least once a day, you are taking action to prevent tartar buildup and tooth decay.

If you do not brush regularly or see a dentist for check-ups and cleanings, you are putting yourself at risk of developing tooth pain that will require an unexpected visit to a dentist. If you do not practice good oral hygiene, a sharp pain from the tooth's nerve can come without warning. When this happens, it is too late to enforce preventative maintenance. What is done is done. Therefore, corrective action at this point would be to see a dentist as soon as possible. Being seen immediately would be wonderful, but this is unlikely to happen, since tooth pain is most likely to strike at the worst possible time.

What if tooth pain strikes when you are on vacation or at another incredibly inconvenient time? In cases like these, your teeth are scheduling you because you did not schedule them for a check-up or take care of them. However, by managing and prioritizing proactive maintenance, you can avoid such emotional discomfort and financial distress and take control of these matters in your life. Consequently, due to poor maintenance habits, your focus shifts to managing the pain.

Scheduling regular dental check-ups can be a source of anxiety, but it's important to remember that they will be less costly and less stressful in the long run. During regular visits, if there is an issue with your teeth, dentists will notice it before it becomes a significant issue. A dentist can remove a small amount of decay in a short visit with only a slight disruption to the natural tooth's contours. Thus, your good habits in preventive maintenance will help avoid many unnecessary, painful, and uncomfortable situations and keep your teeth healthy and your smile looking great.

Let's move on to personal relationships. Just as preventative maintenance is crucial for our health, it's equally important in relationships. The beauty of relationships lies in both parties being good listeners and emotionally available. In a well-balanced relationship, supporting each other becomes a pillar of strength. Like watering a plant is needed for maintenance, expressing gratitude and thankfulness also keeps friendships and relationships fresh. And, of course, keeping the basics in check with regular maintenance is crucial: being honest and open and resolving conflicts fairly.

Maintaining a strong relationship can be difficult. It's unrealistic to expect anyone to be consistently giving and affectionate every single day. We all have those moments when we don't feel up to contributing anything. Furthermore, resolving a disagreement might take longer than we'd like, and using our time and energy can feel exhausting. Yet a relationship may weaken and fade without regular upkeep—like investing personal time and effort.

Before you know it, days turn into weeks and weeks into months, and you find yourself in a struggling friendship or relationship. Knowing this can happen, take my advice: preventative maintenance is the key to healthy living and strong friendships. The long-term benefits of investing in your relationships are immense. A solid and healthy relationship can bring joy, support, and fulfillment to your life. The most straightforward routes to preventive maintenance can be hugs, notes of affection, and simple phrases such as "How are you today?"

My nonprofessional clinical advice for more significant relationship issues is to proactively engage in maintenance before adverse events happen. By addressing problems when they are relatively small, you can effectively put them to rest, relieving potential future stress. This approach empowers you to make decisions that strengthen relationships and friendships, ensuring they stay solid and stable. Keep in mind, maintenance can refer to any aspect that both individuals have agreed is an essential building block of their relationship or friendship.

Recognizing and addressing individual needs is essential in any relationship. For instance, if someone yearns for affection, simple gestures like hugs and kisses can speak volumes. On the other hand, words of affirmation—such as "you're amazing" or "you look fantastic"—may resonate more deeply with another person. If acts of service and quality time are important, one partner should lend a hand with household chores, repairs, or errands when the other is in need. This tailored approach to showing care and attention helps individuals feel understood and valued in the relationship.

A couple of universal preventative maintenance issues in relationships are the lack of time spent together and the inability to address minor problems. By finding ways to spend time together, couples can proactively solve many future problems. Both partners can benefit from connecting at weekly and monthly events to pique their mutual interest. Therefore, prioritizing preventative maintenance in a friendship can significantly contribute to a long-lasting relationship. Remember, the maintenance doesn't have to be a major overhaul; it just needs to be consistent and ongoing.

Now, let's delve into the domain of physical preventative maintenance. Consistent physical movement keeps your muscles active, toned, and flexible. You don't need to push yourself to the point of stress or injury. Simply incorporating physical activity into your daily routine can work wonders. An ideal 30-minute activity that gets your heart rate up is perfect. Remember, staying physically active is one of the most effective ways to improve your health. It will help you avoid unnecessary medical attention.

If you haven't yet made working out a habit, whether through organized sports or outdoor running, it's important to choose activities you genuinely enjoy and can see yourself doing daily. Finding joy in physical activities is a powerful motivator, so they need not be overly strenuous. Think about simple, enjoyable activities like cycling, swimming, slowly jogging, or increasing your activity at work—any movement counts!

The central point of preventative maintenance is to start as soon as possible. It is never too late to support a healthy heart and cardiovascular system. Start by doing some activity in short intervals each day. Then, as the weeks progress, build in more time until you reach 30 minutes a day. It is one of the best ways to live longer and live healthier. If you are healthy now and continue to stay healthy, staying active when you are older will be easier.

If you find yourself straying from your workout routine, don't worry. Life happens, and it can be challenging to stay on track. The important thing is to start again and strive to maintain your workout routine for as many days as possible. Consistency is your best form of preventive maintenance. Remember, staying in motion is easier than getting back into motion. Therefore, if you can keep your routine going without an extended break, keep it going.

Returning to a routine after a long break can be challenging, so you want to avoid long breaks in your preventative maintenance routine. If you find yourself in this situation, one effective strategy is to change your workout routine, which can help you stay motivated and maintain consistency in your daily exercise. Mixing things up keeps boredom at bay and supports a preventive maintenance routine.

A consistent preventative maintenance routine ensures that the essential events and connections you rely on remain in optimal condition. Regularly inspecting, servicing, and addressing potential issues before they escalate can significantly reduce the risk of unexpected losses. With a strong preventative maintenance plan, mechanical things will last longer, your health will be more stable, and your friendships will endure the ups and downs of living life. Your attention to this proactive approach allows you to focus on what truly matters without worrying about interruptions.

Critical Thinking and Self-reliance

A framework of self-reliance, built on the belief in one's capabilities and the confidence to harness them, serves as a powerful tool that empowers individuals to make decisions and take charge of their lives. The journey toward establishing self-reliance nurtures many strong attributes, such as good judgment, self-worth, and self-expression. Self-expression, an essential aspect of self-reliance, allows individuals to effectively communicate their needs, express their desires, and establish personal boundaries, thereby promoting independence and, in turn, self-reliance.

Despite the inherent difficulty in pinpointing the exact characteristics linked to self-reliance, its profound sense of freedom is undeniably real. Individuals who embody self-reliance often exhibit stability, independence, and a proactive approach to problem-solving. These qualities not only license them to navigate life's challenges with confidence but also foster a deep sense of autonomy and self-determination. Ultimately, self-reliance's liberation enables people to pursue their goals and aspirations authentically, unhindered by external pressures or expectations.

While some association exists between a person's independence, it is important not to confuse independence with self-reliance. Self-reliance is about believing in one's ability and having the confidence to see things through, whether it means seeking help from others or allowing others to intervene, which can boost one's confidence. On the other hand, independence may focus entirely on not needing help from others and may have little to do with seeing things through and accomplishing goals. Furthermore, self-reliance is about believing in one's abilities and having the confidence to act on them, while independence is about not relying on others. Therefore, understanding this distinction is key to feeling understood and accepted on your journey to self-reliance.

The self-reliance I am referring to is not about financial stability or about shouldering every hardship. It's about avoiding conformity, being of sound mind, and choosing a path for yourself and following it wherever it may lead. I can tell you right now, this will require critical thinking skills. For instance, when faced with a difficult decision, critical thinking allows you to weigh the pros and cons, consider potential outcomes, and make an informed decision. Critical thinking is a foundational piece of self-reliance. Recognizing the vital importance of critical thinking and its connection to self-reliance can guide you toward greater liberation and greater awareness.

Those who do not spend time thinking critically about significant areas in their life will often follow in the footsteps of others. Hence, following others is easier and more convenient than thinking critically about one's life's mission and forging a personal path. The difference between the two, making your way and following others, is separated by thinking skills cultivated in the practice of self-reliance.

With well-developed thinking skills, you can create and implement your path rather than follow others.

Self-reliance is about trusting your instincts and your ability to think autonomously. It is a feeling of confidence backed by a solid attitude to see things through. Similarly, thinking critically about personal situations and acting on the best possible move go hand in hand with trusting your abilities. A stance of self-reliance shows others you embrace your individuality and are willing to take on unknown variables. As people become more self-reliant, their confidence grows in their ability to think critically about what is happening around them. In this way, critical thinking and self-reliance grow together and support each other, leading to personal growth and development.

Of course, as mentioned earlier, self-reliance does not mean you can go it alone and do not need the support of others. There will be times when you will need the support of others to bridge a gap you cannot possibly make on your own. Accepting support does not mean you are not self-reliant; it means you are thinking critically about your position and recognizing others have resources you do not. Accepting support at crucial moments builds confidence and a stronger sense of self-reliance. Consequently, it's okay to seek help when needed. It's a sign of strength, not weakness.

Critical thinking skills lay the foundation for a strong sense of self-reliance when good choices build on one another. The better choices you make, the more your critical thinking skills improve, which boosts your confidence in your ability to be self-reliant. These two elements work together to help you become the best version of yourself.

If you want to, you can gain self-reliance and some independence. It is not a complicated process. Start by thinking critically about what you want and what you want to do about it. This may take some time and practice, but it's okay if you need help from others to put these early pieces of the puzzle together. Acquiring help from others can answer difficult questions and allow you to gather the resources required to move you from one point to another in your thinking. This process can also help you get started on your self-reliance journey.

Recognizing certain realities, such as the need for help from others and asking questions about things you do not know much about, doesn't undermine your self-reliance; instead, it demonstrates your resourcefulness and understanding that true independence often comes with the need for assistance from others, just as they may rely on your support. As you develop your critical thinking skills, this concept will become more apparent at various stages of your journey toward self-reliance. Lastly, remaining self-reflective and assessing your abilities to prevent arrogance or self-righteousness is crucial. These two mindsets can be significant hurdles in both achieving and sustaining self-reliance.

What is your definition of *self-reliance*? Write it down so you can revisit and reflect on it.

How is *self-reliance* tied to critical thinking?

How has your *self-reliance* (or lack of) impacted your life up to this point?

How do critical thinking skills strengthen a person's sense of *self-reliance*?

Explain how developing a progressive sense of *self-reliance* can positively impact a person's life.

Explain how the absence of developing a sense of *self-reliance* may hurt a person's life. (For instance, avoiding potential dangers, understanding personal emotions, etc.)

Express how you feel about *self-reliance* being one of the most essential things in a successful life. (You may need to define the term successful.)

Chapter 3
Take Your Health Seriously

Time and health are two precious assets that we don't recognize and appreciate until they have been depleted.

— **Denis Waitley**

Life has a way of catching up with us, slowing us down, and reminding us of our mortality, emphasizing that our time is limited. I've noticed I can no longer run as fast or jump as high as I did when I was younger. It's easy to fall into the mindset that life is abundant and that we can keep moving at the same pace we did before, even when we indulge in unhealthy habits. Unfortunately, this isn't the reality. Common unhealthy choices include smoking, heavy drinking, leading a sedentary lifestyle, poor work habits, and a lack of drive to improve our circumstances.

While some decisions you make might not seem directly connected to your physical health, they can significantly impact your mental and emotional well-being. Poor choices can lead to a range of physical, cognitive, and emotional outcomes. No matter the type, these missteps can weigh us down and diminish our overall quality of life. The best direction for yourself and your future is to make healthy choices, especially when your health is already in good shape.

Regardless of age, your ability to make wise decisions is always in your hands. By making positive choices, you can create a path toward a healthier and more rewarding life. As a young adult, you have a unique chance to put your health and well-being first. Although many young adults often neglect their health, the power to make a change is within you. Do not take for granted the power you have to make your life the way you want it. You should also keep in mind that youth is fleeting.

In their youth, individuals often experience rapid healing across physical, mental, and emotional domains and generally bounce back quickly from minor setbacks and injuries. Because time seems plentiful during this stage, young adults may not fully grasp its significance or impact. Instead, they concentrate on immediate wants and desires, giving little thought to how their choices may shape the future. This limited perspective is one of the primary reasons parents and guardians emphasize the importance of youth health. They strive to provide nutritious meals, encourage physical activity, and instill healthy habits, recognizing that such priorities may not be at the forefront of a young person's mind.

I cannot stress this point enough: take care of your health. Since you are reading this book, I assume you are no longer a child. Accordingly, you make choices about your health today that you didn't make as a child. Consequently, you are directly involved in actions that affect your well-being. Therefore, I recommend investing in and maintaining your health. You can achieve this by monitoring your diet, such as opting for whole foods instead of processed ones, and being physically active by exercising regularly instead of sitting and browsing the internet.

Maintaining a healthy lifestyle can be straightforward: focus on eating well and staying physically active. These habits can help you achieve a healthy weight, lower your risk of chronic diseases such as diabetes and heart disease, enhance your mood, and increase your energy levels. Regular exercise also improves sleep quality and helps reduce stress. By making it a habit to eat nutritious foods and exercise consistently, you not only prevent health problems but also set the foundation for a longer life.

Here are some insightful comments you may not have heard that can help you live a healthier life with minimal effort. First, increasing your fiber intake by just ten percent (10%) can reduce ALL mortality factors by fifty percent (50%) and lower the risk of serious diseases. Second, for every pound you lose, you relieve four pounds of pressure on your knees. I encourage you to seek more healthy tips and integrate a few into your daily routine for a better lifestyle.

Don't underestimate health issues, even if they seem trivial at first. You are your own best advocate when it comes to managing your health. Minor symptoms can quickly escalate if left unaddressed. These minor symptoms are subtle signals from your body telling you to slow down or take a breather. Therefore, paying attention to these warning signs and stepping back from major physical activities when signals of poor health arise is always wiser than risking a small problem turning into a major one by continuing a routine. Serious setbacks can result in more daunting challenges and typically require a longer recovery. So, take charge of your health by being proactive and closely monitoring it.

Imagine you suddenly notice something off about your body. It's crucial to dig deeper and understand what's going on. Sometimes, it could be a minor issue you can quickly resolve, letting you return to your usual routine. However, a minor irritation can snowball into a significant problem if unchecked. The best action is to keep minor issues small by investigating them early. Don't let minor physical concerns go unattended; they can develop into significant problems.

A friend of mine was passionate about running long distances during her workouts. She dedicated herself to training for half marathons and ran several each year. However, one day, she began feeling discomfort in her shin. Sometimes the irritation would lessen during a run, but it would return the next day. She didn't pay much attention since it wasn't a constant problem. She felt no urgency to address the issue immediately and continued her workout routine, running a few times a week. Since it only occasionally bothered her, she thought she could adjust her pace and stride to cover up the irritability.

Weeks later, the irritation worsened, and she suspected it was shin splints, a common condition among runners caused by overusing the lower leg muscles. After taking a couple of weeks off from running, the pain subsided. However, when she resumed her regular running routine, she experienced sharp pain in her shin during a lighter workout.

She immediately stopped, sat down to relieve the pain, and waited for it to subside before attempting to walk home.

The following day, after visiting her doctor, she learned that her injury was a stress fracture caused by repetitive high-impact exercise. The doctor advised her to rest adequately and to stop running for at least three months. If her condition does not improve, she may need to consider surgery.

My friend's story serves as a cautionary tale. She ignored the early signs of her health issues, which ultimately led to a more severe diagnosis. Her options for recovery were a three-month break from running or to undergo surgery. The solutions might have been much less drastic if she had sought medical attention for her shin pain sooner. Early detection and care could have been as simple as wearing proper footwear, periodically replacing her running shoes, or modifying her exercise routine through cross-training. Instead, she chose the more challenging path to recovery by overlooking the initial signs of her health concerns.

As an individual engaged in physical activities, you play a crucial role in managing your health. It is important to monitor your health regularly and address any issues promptly. For this reason, here are some important points that doctors and professional trainers want you to consider when taking your health seriously.

First, avoid doing too much too quickly. Overexertion can lead to injuries such as muscle strains, stress fractures, respiratory issues, and heart problems. When exercising, focus on gradually increasing the duration and weight of your activities. Give your body time to adjust to the added stress. For instance, if you're running, aim to increase your mileage and intensity by no more than ten percent every couple of weeks. This allows your body to slowly build the muscles needed to run longer distances. This gradual approach to gaining strength and stamina will help you during future workouts.

Second, it's crucial to avoid running, playing, or lifting weights if you're experiencing pain. Recognize the difference between normal muscle soreness, a natural part of building muscle, and pain, which can indicate a more serious issue. Many people ignore the warning signs of their health, but it is crucial to their well-being not to overlook these indicators. Therefore, take the time to identify and address the issues before they worsen.

Pain is typically a sign that should not be ignored, as it rarely resolves on its own without intervention. Taking proactive steps to address the underlying issue is crucial for recovery. It is important to recognize that pain functions as a fundamental warning mechanism, indicating that your body may require rest or, in some cases, prompt medical evaluation. By developing an awareness of your body and being attuned to its signals, you can better respond to these discomforts with appropriate measures—whether that involves seeking professional guidance, adjusting your activities, or implementing self-care practices. Listening to your body is not only vital for alleviating current issues but also for preventing future complications.

Conversely, muscle aches and irritability are crucial indicators that your body is signaling for support and recovery. When experiencing these symptoms, simple yet effective recovery methods, such as applying ice to the affected areas and ensuring you get plenty of rest, are advisable. Additionally, it may be beneficial to reassess your workout technique. Consider using lighter weights or performing fewer repetitions to give your body the time it needs to heal.

While adjusting your routine, it's helpful to visualize the process of working out and recuperating as the construction of a house. Just as a building requires a strong foundation to ensure stability and longevity, your body also requires optimal health to support your fitness endeavors. If you continue to exert yourself through strenuous exercise without addressing underlying health concerns, the overall structure of your physical well-being may become unstable. Therefore, prioritizing self-care and giving your body the time it needs to recover is essential for achieving sustainable health and fitness.

It's beneficial to incorporate cross-training activities that engage various muscle groups to boost your fitness routine and minimize muscle fatigue. Cross-training allows some muscles to rest while others are working. For example, if you primarily run for exercise, your legs endure a lot of impact while your upper body experiences minimal impact.

By adding swimming to your workout regimen, you can give your legs a break, as swimming targets upper-body muscles. Thus, combining running and swimming enables you to exercise your legs in one activity and your upper body in another, promoting overall muscle balance and reducing fatigue.

Other examples of cross-training activities include cycling, yoga, and strength training. For example, consider adding a yoga session after a long run to help stretch and relax your muscles. Alternatively, you can focus on upper-body strength training on days when you're not running. The basic concept of cross-training is to allow one muscle group to rest (not work as hard) while another is working harder. This approach helps maintain good overall health by preventing continuous strain on a single muscle group, which can lead to fatigue and injury.

Let's examine the difference between 'hurt' and 'pain.' 'Hurt' describes a general sense of discomfort, whereas 'pain' signifies actual physical damage to the body. Injuries such as 'hurt' can result from direct contact in various scenarios, including participating in competitive sports, experiencing vehicle collisions, or engaging in outdoor activities like running on uneven trails.

Experiencing hurt or pain after an incident is often understandable and sometimes unavoidable. Certain activities, especially in sports, can lead to injuries that cause pain or discomfort. For this reason, athletes who participate in a particular sport are aware of what causes their pain, which is a good head start in knowing how it occurred and what needs to be done to recover. For instance, athletes may sustain injuries from tackles, falls, or collisions with other players, leading to sprains, fractures, or bruises. Similarly, in the unfortunate event of a car accident, individuals may suffer from whiplash, broken bones, or concussions due to the force of the impact. Additionally, trail runners might twist an ankle while navigating rocky terrain or encountering sudden elevation changes, which can lead to sprains or strains. While I sincerely hope you never find yourself in any of these situations, it's crucial to be aware of the potential risks and to take necessary precautions to stay safe.

On the other hand, pain occurs on a deeper level and suddenly surfaces without warning. Therefore, if you experience discomfort or 'pain,' you should have things checked out. Pain does not necessarily occur only due to contact, such as in sports. Examples include tooth pain when the nerve is sensitive or sunburn when the skin has been exposed to excessive radiation. In most cases of pain, seeking medical attention is crucial to prevent further damage and ensure proper healing.

Even if you understand exactly what caused an accident, it's essential to recognize that it's still an unintended incident. Taking the necessary time to heal, recover, and move forward is important in these situations. Moreover, it's crucial to have any injuries checked out by a doctor to rule out any serious underlying problems.

Seeking medical attention for your injuries is not a sign of weakness; it's a proactive step towards your long-term well-being. When recovering from injuries (hurts) or pain, following a physical therapy plan is important, even if the plan is to stop doing what caused the injury. A significant point to remember is that neglecting a recovery plan can lead to lifelong regret. Therefore, do not underestimate the seriousness of injuries.

It's common to feel invincible when young; younger bodies heal faster than older ones. However, this won't always be the case. Therefore, as life progresses, it's important to establish a routine for maintaining your health. The human body slows down its healing process with age, meaning that an injury experienced in youth can have long-lasting effects if not adequately treated. By developing healthy habits as a young adult, you can take control of your health and ensure a brighter future. Cultivating healthy habits in your youth is essential as time passes quickly.

Before you know it, a few decades will pass, and you will feel much older and heal much more slowly. If you don't believe me, think back on your life as a first grader. As a young adult now, that was a decade or two ago, and it has flown by. The next decade or two will pass quickly as well. You won't even notice it because you will be busy with various activities that take up your time, such as attending college, working, building friendships, being in relationships, and dealing with family matters. Time proceeds quickly and relentlessly; therefore, you must make a conscious effort to foster a healthier future by prioritizing your health and preventing injuries. Remember, your health is not something you can buy later.

This chapter on health vigilance is significant when the cause of an injury is unknown. Therefore, if you begin to feel discomfort but are unsure of its origin (how it happened), it's essential to investigate rather than dismiss it, hoping it will resolve on its own. Taking proactive steps can help prevent minor issues from escalating. If the discomfort persists, it warrants further examination. For example, if a body part is hurting and you can't recall how it happened, don't think of it as trivial; it might not be. Take time to investigate and ask a medical professional questions to better understand the source of the ache or pain.

Address issues when they are small and relatively easy to manage. For example, if you experience wrist pain, you might find out that you have a form of carpal tunnel syndrome. This condition occurs when the median nerve at the wrist is compressed, causing pain. It commonly affects individuals who engage in repetitive hand movements, such as cashiers, typists, carpenters, assembly workers, and athletes. While carpal tunnel syndrome is typically associated with adults, it can also develop at a younger age. Remember, even severe conditions like carpal tunnel syndrome can be effectively managed with early intervention.

Let me share a story about how cross-training led to a healthier future. I worked as a cashier at a supermarket for twelve years. This job involves repetitive wrist movements, which can lead to carpal tunnel syndrome, characterized by numbness, tingling, and pain in the hand and arm. I knew several cashiers who had experienced this issue.

I remember a few cashiers complaining of wrist aches, often dismissing them as a regular part of a long workday. They would rub the affected wrist area, and sometimes the pain would subside temporarily. However, the discomfort worsened over time, prompting a career change.

I never experienced the same level of development as others, even though I performed the same repetitive movements day after day. I attribute my success to cross-training. Playing tennis regularly helped strengthen the muscles in my wrist, rather than overworking a single muscle group as I would have by only working as a cashier. By incorporating tennis workouts, I could support the muscles that typically would have been strained due to carpal tunnel syndrome.

Switching gears but staying on the topic of 'health,' let's explore ways to enhance your academic health by prioritizing your well-being in your educational endeavors. Achieving greater academic stability requires your grades to reflect your true potential. While you know you can accomplish more, you might be struggling to find the motivation to put in the necessary effort. If the idea of being in school feels uninspiring or if you're struggling to understand assignments and meet deadlines, these may signal that it's time to reach out for assistance. Remember, seeking help is a sign of strength and can significantly improve your academic health.

When physical movement causes pain, it signals the beginning of an issue related to that activity. If you experience discomfort during physical activity, it's vital to investigate the cause, address it, and continue. Similarly, if you are struggling academically, you should explore why. Understanding why is crucial if you're not enjoying learning or caring about your future. Simply dismissing your academic struggles as indifference towards the class or the material won't help. Uncovering the root causes of your challenges can increase your engagement and enhance the health of your academic future.

Your academic 'health' will not improve unless you actively investigate the issues associated with it. However, failing to do so will only lead to more significant difficulties. Keep in mind that every course you take plays a vital role in shaping your overall grade and showcases your ability to handle your workload effectively. Crafting a clear academic plan for success—much like a roadmap for your journey in physical therapy—is essential. Demonstrating that you grasp this concept shows your potential to excel in your academic journey.

Your feelings about being in school, performing well on assignments, and taking academic challenges will improve if you take them seriously, especially when you seek help. If you are disengaged from your education, explore why you prefer to avoid school or learning. Consider discussing your feelings with a teacher or visiting a counselor for guidance. Sometimes, the simple act of discussing issues with others can lead to resolutions. Understanding your academic health involves recognizing your strengths and weaknesses, seeking assistance, and working diligently to improve your performance.

Ask yourself why you feel unmotivated about laying the foundation for your future. It's important to realize that your academic performance significantly impacts your opportunities for higher education and your career prospects outside secondary education. Although doing well in life and achieving some recognition for your efforts may seem like a distant dream while you are in school, it's a tangible reality that your actions can create during your time in secondary education. It's important to tackle any issues before they escalate and become more significant challenges that could create obstacles you find difficult to navigate.

Working through educational challenges is meant to establish a motivation structure within you that will help you achieve your goals later in life. When approached correctly and with the right attitude, this drive to succeed can foster a willingness to take on new experiences. Examine your academic performance and determine why you lack motivation. Identify any issues and consider ways to resolve them. A lack of motivation to build a solid foundation for your future and an unwillingness to recognize the benefits of hard work can lead to an unhealthy future.

If you explore the reasons behind your lack of motivation in school and address those underlying 'injuries' (metaphorically speaking), you will prevent them from becoming more significant problems. By doing so, you will be setting yourself up for a healthier future. The effort you invest now will contribute to your success and well-being down the line. Don't let today's frustrations, hurts, and pains carry over into tomorrow. Prioritize your health in all physical, emotional, spiritual, relational, or educational areas.

Chapter 4
Mentors Move You from Good to Great

Listen to your elder's advice, not because they are always right but because they have more experiences of being wrong.

— MS Dhoni

My friends, to be an individual and to be different from others is the only way to become distinguished from the common herd. Be glad, we are different from one another in form and in deposition. Variety is the spice of life, and we are various enough to enjoy one another's society; so, let us be content and learn from one another as we live.

— **modified from L Frank Baun**

Mentors can enhance your skills from good to great. When looking for a mentor, identify your goals and the areas you seek to improve. Next, look for individuals who have achieved similar goals or possess relevant expertise. Reach out to them, explain your situation, and ask if they would be willing to mentor you. All it takes is your genuine effort to improve.

Honest and reliable mentors are exceptionally skilled at helping their mentees avoid significant issues, obstacles, and stumbling blocks. Although mentors cannot predict the future, they can lead, guide, and support you in the present to help shape your future. With the support of a mentor, navigating hindrances and setbacks with prior understanding and resolving them early on makes the path to success more effortless, making your journey more rewarding and enjoyable.

Having a mentor in your life is a great way to accomplish more in less time. Mentors are not just sounding boards; they are pillars of support, willing to listen to you explain your struggles, frustrations, and joys of accomplishments. They provide helpful advice, making goals more attainable and realistic. They also offer emotional support to navigate feelings of confusion. Therefore, you will accomplish more in less time with the added understanding and clarity. If it sounds too good to be true, it's because it is. Nothing is this easy.

Mentors can nurture you from a poor position to a better one or from a low point to a higher point. The shift from a problematic situation to a more stable position, or from a low point to a high one, hinges on your ability to take control. Hence, you are not just your biggest obstacle but also your most significant catalyst when achieving your goals. No mentor can force you to listen to them if you choose not to. On the other hand, if you decide to listen, no one can force you to act on their advice except you. Mentors can be invaluable, but their effectiveness is directly proportional to your willingness to act on their advice.

Your active participation in the mentoring process is not just crucial; it's essential. Your participation ensures that the advice you receive is not just heard but implemented. Your drive is the catalyst that transforms your performance from good to great. Numerous individuals have achieved remarkable feats by excelling in their fields of interest. However, the ones who truly stand out are those who seek guidance from seasoned mentors and act on it. Heeding and translating mentors' advice into action can elevate a person from good to great. Hence, the profound impact of mentors on a person's life boils down to the fundamental principles of active listening and proactive implementation.

A mentor can offer a wealth of wisdom and compelling reasons to pursue your goals. They can also provide invaluable insights to steer clear of potential pitfalls. However, their guidance will only take you so far if you do not integrate their knowledge and wisdom into your actions. Consequently, you must incorporate their teachings into your routines to benefit from their experience and wisdom. Thus, the entire mentoring process hinges on one pivotal question: Are you ready to transform a mentor's advice into tangible results?

Making your way through life can be exciting. Many rites of passage and significant milestones mark your transition from one life stage to another. Some of these rites of passage are owning a vehicle and attending higher education. Both develop lasting independence and capitalize on significant opportunities. Other important rites of passage are entering the military, getting married, seeing parts of the world, and starting a business. All these build character way beyond those who do not attempt them.

Consider rites of passage as personal journeys. These experiences can be like exploring an unknown path or traveling down an unfamiliar road. Your experiences will be uniquely yours, even if you have companions with you. Every experience you encounter will be uniquely yours, shaped by your perceptions and emotions, even when friends or family surround you. Whether shared or solitary, each moment will resonate with your unique perspective, creating memories that reflect your journey.

Regarding certain rites of passage, you should team up with a friend to navigate the ups and downs together. On the other hand, there may be instances where you choose to strike out on your own. Remember that you will face new and unfamiliar challenges, as these journeys often come with their own set of hurdles. Many of these unknowns can feel overwhelming, such as managing your finances, asserting your independence, resolving conflicts, and tackling unexpected situations.

These are the challenges that a mentor can help you navigate, making the journey less daunting and more rewarding. Receiving support from mentors in all these areas will always be a personal gain. The better news is that working through the unknowns often builds character and grit, helping you become more resilient. However, these obstacles may also leave you feeling disappointed and discouraged, to the point where you want to give up. This is why mentors are worth their weight in gold. Mentors support your efforts as you journey. Mentors want to see you succeed and experience as little discouragement and disappointment as possible.

Your goal should be to reach the finish line of your goals and dreams while gaining invaluable experience. Mentors support this process. Additionally, sharing these experiences with others is important, as you can guide and help those just starting their journey, continuing the mentorship and personal growth cycle. By sharing your experiences, you contribute to others' growth and become part of a supportive community that celebrates everyone's success and overcomes challenges together. This sense of connection and shared success makes mentorship genuinely fulfilling.

When I use the word mentor, I refer to someone you admire and trust. A mentor is someone you look up to who gives you good advice—advice you genuinely respect and can utilize to accomplish your goals. You should trust this person to be on your side, and you have no doubt they care for you. This is an important concept because you may not like or want their advice, but if you trust the person giving it, you will incorporate it into your life even though you may not see its relevance at the time.

A mentor worthy of your time is someone you will take advice from and follow because you know it is in your best interest. This trust and acceptance of advice can empower you in your personal and professional growth, giving you a sense of control and direction. Trusting your mentor is essential, as your progress relies on heeding their advice and wisdom. Furthermore, believing in them is crucial because a lot of what your future will be based on comes from listening to and acting on their words and wisdom.

That being said, allowing a mentor in your life can be challenging. Not everyone can do it. Acting on another person's advice and putting their words to good use can be difficult. This is because people, by nature, are individualistic and want to make their own decisions. Seldom do individuals allow others to make decisions that affect their lives. The basic reason for this is people have likes and dislikes. They know what makes them comfortable and what makes them uncomfortable. Consequently, making decisions on one's own behalf is much easier than taking advice from others.

Decisions based on personal preferences prevent individuals from stepping too far outside their comfort zones. Consequently, mentors' advice may do precisely this: push a person out of their comfort zone. The benefit is that stepping out of a comfort zone by accepting advice can lead to significant personal growth. Ideally, this growth can inspire those receiving advice to reach new heights and realize their full potential. It's important to emphasize that striving for excellence, even beyond one's personal preferences, can be challenging. Thus, it is difficult to incorporate others' advice into your plans, as it may conflict with your preferences.

Many people think their ideas and approaches are the most effective way to reach their goals. This mindset explains why they might view following someone else's advice as a waste of time. Additionally, many find it challenging to accept help from others because they want to demonstrate they can accomplish things independently. Additionally, acknowledging the need for support can be seen as a sign of dependence rather than independent success. If you find yourself in these mindsets, seek assistance from those more successful than you and gradually increase your acceptance of their advice.

I mention this because your perspectives on independence reflect a common mindset of someone striving to achieve their goals solo, often without awareness of the challenges that may arise. This independent and isolated mindset tends to characterize someone navigating their path alone. While I understand that these views can be valid and valuable, they frequently result in being good at what you do rather than great. Conversely, paying attention to a mentor's guidance can elevate you from merely good to greatness. The difference between the two lies in a dynamic exchange in which advice, knowledge, and experience enrich one another, leading to profound personal growth.

Based on my experience, those who embrace their mentors' advice and actively apply it tend to exceed their goals and expectations. Hence, mentors are crucial for navigating challenges, preventing disappointments, and setbacks. As I mentioned, you already possess the tools to succeed in whatever you pursue. However, these tools need to be paired with your drive, desire, and the guidance you receive from your mentor. A mentor can illuminate the path forward, but it's up to you to take the first steps and move along that path.

Most people go it alone and achieve what they can, however they can. With this route, things either turn out okay or not at all. Don't be like these others who settle for just okay or for a goal that does not fully materialize. Find a mentor you admire and respect, one who values you and what you are trying to accomplish. Then, incorporate their life lessons into your life and achieve great things. Mentors can move you from good to great if you are willing to work at it.

Critical Thinking and Kindness

The interpretation of kindness varies significantly among individuals, as its meaning is influenced by the context and manner in which it is expressed. For instance, kindness can take many forms, from simple assistance to a deeply emotional gesture, yet its essence remains subjective. Similarly, the notion of being 'nice' can be perceived through different lenses, heavily dependent on the delivery and sincerity behind the words or actions.

Sometimes, being nice may be interpreted as a deception, particularly when an individual resorts to exaggerated politeness to conceal their genuine emotions or opinions. This perception arises because being nice often involves maintaining charity and adhering to social norms. Consequently, this can lead to a situation in which being 'nice' is equated with levity; it may come across as merely meeting the minimum expectations of social interaction rather than an authentic expression of goodwill.

At its core, the distinction between kindness and niceness lies in the depth of genuine intentions and the complexity of the human emotions that underlie each interaction. Kindness often involves a heartfelt desire to uplift others, characterized by empathy, compassion, and a willingness to engage in acts that genuinely benefit someone. In contrast, niceness can sometimes be superficial, arising from social norms or a desire to be liked, without necessarily reflecting a genuine emotional connection. Therefore, the nuances of these two concepts reveal how our heartfelt actions and thoughtful interactions can significantly impact others' lives, underscoring the importance of authenticity in our relationships.

Thus, kindness is not just about actions but about their emotional impact. A true sense of sincerity identifies it, which is a more accurate gauge of this attribute. Sincerity is a behavior that expresses a purposeful intent to care for another's feelings and position. Hence, kindness embodies an emotional impact, a powerful force that can uplift the recipient. In many instances, genuine kindness doesn't rely on reciprocation. This means that we shouldn't expect the same in return when we show kindness to others. Consequently, kindness can be seen as a one-way street; it represents a sincere expression of care and concern for others without expecting something in return.

Can you recall a time when you wanted to pay forward a kind act someone did for you? I remember when a stranger helped me carry a large item to my car while I struggled to manage. This act of kindness made me want to do something kind for someone else. Events like this embody the concept of kindness as a 'one-way street.' In similar circumstances, kindness reflects the goodwill we've received from others. When someone feels grateful, they're often driven to pay that kindness forward. Thus, genuine kindness moves in one direction, outward as it is shared freely with those around us.

If genuine kindness were not a 'one-way street' and the giver expected something in return, the act of kindness might end. The process would cease, and the cycle would be disrupted if a kind act were expected to be reciprocated by the giver. However, since there are other avenues of returning kindness besides directly to the giver, such as paying it forward by helping a stranger or volunteering in a community, there is a higher likelihood that someone's thankfulness will be expressed to a third party.

Thus, one small act of kindness is felt throughout an entire community through the ripple effect of 'one-way street' acts of kindness. One person is doing something kind to another, and that person is doing something kind for someone else. Creating this collage of paying kindness forward establishes a pattern of thinking critically about one's actions based on experiences.

When we think critically about our actions and those of others, we understand that we all have moments of greatness and failure. In reflection, we realize that kindness is a choice, as we critically examine how others handle life's obstacles. Hence, it's within our power to display kindness where we see the need. Kindness is more than being nice; it's about self-improvement and self-reflection. Critical thinking is a skill that supports our giving to others through kindness and our self-improvement through self-reflection.

There is a difference between 'nice' and 'kind'. Being nice is like standing far from someone who can use help and having the capacity to support them. In contrast, kindness is taking a closer and more personal view of the situation and becoming concerned about the person by getting involved. The difference between the two, being nice (friendly) and being kind (involved), is that they are separated by critical thinking and the decision to support others in need. Furthermore, kindness promotes higher-level thinking by diving deeper into others' feelings and fostering a willingness to meet their needs where they are.

What is your definition of *kindness*? Write it down so you can revisit and reflect on it.

How is *kindness* tied to critical thinking?

How has your k*indness* (or lack of) impacted your life up to this point?

How do critical thinking skills strengthen a person's sense of *kindness*?

Explain how developing a progressive sense of *kindness* can positively impact a person's life.

Explain how the absence of developing a sense of *kindness* may hurt a person's life. (For instance, avoiding potential dangers, understanding personal emotions, etc.)

Express how you feel about *kindness* being one of the most essential things in a successful life. (You may need to define the term successful)

Chapter 5
Stay Calm in Adversity

Everything You've Ever Wanted is on the Other Side of Fear.

— **George Addair**

'Staying calm' is not just a state of mind but a crucial factor in making sound decisions. Therefore, staying calm should be considered essential when dealing with life's challenges, such as job loss, broken relationships, low academic performance, or unexpected traffic jams. Other situations that can be equally stressful and require staying calm include public speaking, financial difficulties, health issues, and family conflicts.

Remaining calm facilitates better decision-making, which often leads to more favorable outcomes. On the other hand, losing composure in stressful situations often leads to poor decisions and adverse outcomes. Moreover, remaining calm and making well-thought-out decisions are essential for navigating challenging financial, emotional, social, and spiritual situations. Therefore, staying calm and creating a plan is always the best choice.

Stress can significantly affect your ability to remain calm when faced with challenges or when your livelihood is threatened. To effectively manage stress in these situations, it's important to stay composed, create a plan, and implement it. But how can you stay calm when stress feels so overwhelming? One practical and effective approach is to practice mindfulness, which involves focusing on the present moment and accepting it without judgment.

Mindfulness, practiced without judgment, invites individuals to notice their thoughts, emotions, and sensations as they come up. This approach fosters a deeper insight into their automatic responses and patterns, enhancing self-awareness and understanding. By promoting this awareness, a person can develop greater emotional resilience and clarity, reducing stress and improving overall quality of life. Integrating mindfulness into daily routines, whether through meditation, mindful breathing, or simply pausing to notice the environment, can create a profound shift in how a person experiences each moment and help calm the body's physiological response to stress.

As you may already know, the body's response to stress is a complex and powerful mechanism. Understanding this process can empower you to take control of your responses in stressful situations. When stress triggers the body's fight-or-flight mode, the mind signals the body to prepare for a physical response. The body produces a stress hormone called cortisol from the adrenal glands. Cortisol then enters the brain and slows the prefrontal cortex, which is responsible for critical thinking and executive functions. This slowdown in brain function can negatively affect your decision-making, underscoring the importance of managing stress effectively.

Scientific research has established a direct correlation between the intensity of hippocampal shrinkage and the rational thinking process. Therefore, understanding how immediate stress and anxiety can impede decision-making is not just informative; it's empowering. Consider a tense situation: confronting a wild animal in the wilderness or an intruder in your home. In tense encounters, the amygdala, a part of the brain, takes over, and the hippocampus narrows, potentially leading to a fight-or-flight response. This narrowing of the hippocampus is linked to cognitive decline.

Knowing these internal processes can help you feel confident that maintaining control over your responses in stressful situations—by focusing on staying calm—will lead to better decision-making. Thus, reacting emotionally or erratically in challenging conditions is not advisable. Consequently, composure will enable you to regain control of a situation quickly and to think more sensibly about better alternatives. In life-threatening events, your best chance of survival is to keep your emotions in check.

Staying calm in adversity is not a skill limited to specific environmental scenarios. It's a skill that can be applied in every situation, whether in civilian life or the wild. Whether you're unexpectedly asked to give a speech in front of strangers or find yourself lost in the woods, staying calm is the key. Implementing the concept of staying calm as a coping strategy can empower you to face any situation with confidence and control, knowing that you have a reliable tool at your disposal.

Staying calm cannot be overstated, as it offers numerous benefits. The phrase 'be calm, cool, and collected' is more than just a saying; it's a strategy for navigating life's challenges. In many situations, maintaining your composure can significantly change the outcome of a potentially dire situation. Therefore, the basic phrase 'stay calm,' along with the others associated with it, should remind you to maintain your composure when faced with challenges. It's not just a saying; it's a powerful tool for managing stress and making better decisions.

For instance, imagine a scenario where you're in a heated argument with a colleague at work. If you let your emotions take over, the situation could escalate and lead to a negative outcome. However, if you stay calm and approach the problem with a logical and sensible mindset, you can find a solution and prevent further damage to your professional relationship. One way to stay calm in such a situation is to slow the conversation and remind yourself to listen before responding. This can help you maintain a level head and respond thoughtfully rather than reactively.

In a job interview, for instance, maintaining your composure can significantly improve your ability to answer questions, create a strong impression, boost confidence, and feel better prepared. This principle also applies to situations like encountering a surprise quiz in class or an unexpected performance review at work. While panic often clouds judgment and leads to poor decisions, staying calm enables you to think clearly and regain a logical perspective.

Applying a logical perspective to situations and returning to a safer mental environment will lower anxiety and stress, thus leading to better thinking and more creative and manageable responses. This process alone will strengthen your cognitive thinking and help you make better judgments about your events. Thinking logically and sensibly creates opportunities to improve a situation, whereas the others, being emotional and unpredictable, do not.

When facing an unexpected crisis, finding reasonable, logical ways to cool down is your best way to navigate it. Once you've regained your composure, it's crucial to devise a plan. This plan should outline steps to tackle the immediate crisis and strategies to prevent similar situations in the future. Acting on this plan will help you regain emotional control and feel more empowered amid the chaos.

When I emphasize discovering an opportunity to cool down is your most effective strategy, it's important to note that this process can occur within mere seconds or may take several minutes, depending on the specific circumstances you're facing. Whether taking a brief pause to breathe deeply, stepping outside for fresh air, or engaging in a calming activity, the time required to regain composure varies significantly based on your emotional state and the situation's intensity. Recognizing when to cool down, devising a plan, and acting on it can lead to better decision-making.

As a young adult, impetuous moments can happen often, so there are a few scenarios where calm, cool, and collected will be your best option. One significant situation is while driving. Road rage can quickly bring on the fight-or-flight response, a natural reaction to perceived threats. This response can lead to poor decision-making and aggressive behavior. The fight-or-flight response is a physiological reaction to a perceived threat to survival. It prepares the body to either fight or flee the danger. For example, if you feel threatened by another driver's actions while driving, your first cognitive reaction would be to retaliate (fight response) or quickly drive away (flight response).

Even as an adult, I have been in this situation and forced into a fight-or-flight response. I did my best to de-escalate the situation by asserting my presence without building up anxiety. However, a while after the incident, I reflected on the ordeal and realized I could have taken many other flight responses, which would have been much better in the long run. That said, developing a calm attitude and working to remain relaxed in chaotic situations will help you assess challenging conditions more effectively, helping you avoid hasty decisions you might later regret.

Using the scenario of road rage and the fight-or-flight response associated with it, you could cause damage to your vehicle and/or cause injuries to yourself and others if poor decisions are made in haste. The best option when someone initiates road rage is to remain calm and defuse the situation by avoiding gestures toward the other driver, such as shaking your fist, flashing your headlights, or making eye contact. Allow the other person to pass by if needed and put distance between you and them. Staying calm in situations such as this will help you think of different ways to resolve these issues with other drivers who are agitated and taking it out on you. Most importantly, acting calmly and rationally will ensure your safety on the road.

Shifting focus while remaining on the topic, it's clear that successful individuals tend to make quick decisions about their desires and are slow to change their minds. In contrast, many unsuccessful people take a long time to figure out what they want and are quick to change direction. This suggests that successful people are more composed, taking the time to carefully assess situations before acting, whereas unsuccessful individuals often react impulsively, lacking a solid plan. As a result, it becomes clear that staying calm and creating a plan leads to greater success than acting impulsively and without direction.

A successful entrepreneur might promptly decide to invest in a new business opportunity because they have a clear strategy and are confident in their ability to execute it. However, unsuccessful people generally lack a plan when issues arise. They debate an issue for a long time, trying to devise a plan at the last minute, only to change it quickly after it is put into action because they are still unsure. Therefore, my advice to you, in whatever situation you find yourself in, business or friendship, is to stay calm, formulate a plan, and be ready to implement it. This will help you avoid the pitfalls of indecisiveness and impulsive actions that often lead to poor results.

It should be noted that having a plan doesn't guarantee that stressful moments will not occur. Stressful moments do not stay away because you have a plan. However, having a plan 'on the ready' increases the likelihood that you will either be prepared for the unexpected or have the foresight to avoid adverse events when and if they arise.

'Plan the dive and dive the plan' is a common saying among scuba divers. It reminds them of the importance of preparation and sticking to a plan. Scuba divers rarely, if ever, are caught off guard. Their lives depend on being prepared. By diving according to their plan, they remain calm. They know the limits they have set for themselves, and they stick to that plan. Deviating from the plan would jeopardize them, and they want to avoid that at all costs.

Scuba divers are adventurous people who provide a great example of staying calm and adhering to a plan. They are laser-focused on their goal of returning to the surface unharmed, and in this regard, divers genuinely understand the value of staying calm under pressure. Using a depth chart and decompression table, they account for their dive time, oxygen consumption rate, and leveling-off zones when resurfacing. Divers understand everything will work well if they stay calm, breathe normally, and follow their dive plan. We can all learn a thing or two from scuba divers. Stay calm, formulate a plan, and let everything else take a backseat.

Another critical key to remaining calm in stressful situations is to adapt to your surroundings as soon as possible. Plans work well when you can carry them out as intended, or when you can formulate a simple one in the moment to see you through a difficult situation; however, plans can change along the way and require you to adjust them to avoid incidents or harm. Those who can adapt rapidly, gather information quickly, and start thinking will emerge victorious over those who resist, deny, and fight their situation.

This adaptability is not just a survival strategy but also a powerful tool for taking control of your circumstances. When kayakers are pulled from their kayak and spun wildly in a 'hydraulic' (the result of rushing water over an object), the best course of action is to relax and let their body sink downward deeper toward the riverbed. The undercurrent at the river floor will push them to calmer waters downstream. If they struggle and resist the force of the rapids, they naturally take bigger breaths, keeping lots of air in their lungs, and thus remain buoyant on the river's surface while the more raging rapids pound them. This is not something they want to do.

Staying calm and exhaling some air from the lungs will naturally have them sink downward into calmer water below, where the current on the riverbed will push them away from the hydraulic. They will resurface downstream.

Thinking back on a personal experience of keeping my cool during tough times, I recall how important it was when I got lost while hiking on a mountain. Staying calm in that moment made all the difference. It took place on Mt. St. Helens one summer long ago. I was trail running and wanted to explore the top of the mountain. I reached the summit and spent a few moments soaking in the breathtaking view. Afterward, I decided to go back down the trail toward the parking lot. After walking back down for a while, I knew something was wrong. Within an hour, I realized I was lost. The beauty of the landscape had captivated me, and I had missed the trail bend needed to descend the mountain safely to the parking lot.

I was way off course. Nothing looked familiar, and my stress and anxiety levels rose quickly. I looked up at the mountain and realized I had no energy to return to the top to find the correct path. I was exhausted and had used up all the water I had brought. With the summer sun beating down, I was quickly becoming dehydrated. I had no idea where I was on the mountain or how lost I was. The foliage surrounding me was about my height, so seeing anything 10 yards in front of me wasn't easy.

The first thing that came to my mind was that a wild animal would attack me, or I would succumb to dehydration and cramp up, forcing me to spend the night without shelter or any form of protection against the elements. The second thought was the most useful— to remain calm. I needed to think about survival and formulate a plan to get out of the situation I got myself into. So, I did. I stayed calm.

I prioritized first things first. I needed to find shade from the hot sun. I needed to rest my hands, which were visibly scraped and sore from climbing on volcanic pumice rocks. I did find some shade. I crouched near a large boulder, the size of a medium truck, and sat in its shade. I sat in the boulder's shade and thought of ways to escape this mess. Then, it dawned on me that if I could locate other hikers, I could follow them off the mountain. That was the plan: find others descending and follow them.

I stared at the top of the mountain and thought, if I could see any movement, it would most likely be a hiker. If I did notice a hiker's movement, I could travel laterally across the mid-section of the mountain in their direction until I met up with the trail they were descending on. It was my only plan, so that's what I did. I stared at the top of the mountain while hiding from the sun's heat in the shade of the large boulder. I fixed my gaze on the top of the mountain for at least twenty minutes, hoping to see any movement. And in that moment of hope, I felt renewed optimism and belief that I could find my way back. Just the idea of having a plan gave me hope.

As I fixed my gaze on the mountaintop, my heart raced as I spotted movement. Something was gradually descending the mountain. I reassured myself it must be hikers making their way down. Two tiny dots were slowly moving down from the top. The size and shape of the little dots in the distance appeared and disappeared with the foliage they were passing. Seeing two small dots in the vastness slowly move downward relative to their background was an incredible sight.

I left the shade of the boulder and began my ascent, moving upward and laterally across the mountain toward the dots' movement. The plan was to intersect their vertical path as they descended from the mountaintop. And it worked. It was a moment of optimism that I will never forget. Although I was not out of danger then, the thought of having a plan and carrying it out gave me enough strength to continue. It was a grueling couple of hours working my way over rugged terrain toward them, but I found the path they descended and made it off the mountain. I am alive today because I stayed composed when I realized I was in a difficult situation.

The plan was simple, but it didn't need to be complicated. I created it to instill hope and shift my focus away from feeling stranded. You can do the same when life presents challenges. Many obstacles may seem like towering, unyielding mountains that are impossible to navigate, but you can overcome them if you remain composed, create a plan, and put in the effort. The sense of accomplishment from overcoming a challenge is inspiring and should motivate you to face your difficulties head-on.

Take professional athletes, for example. The successful ones are good examples of being calm under pressure. Think of Michael Jordan, who famously sank a winning shot in the 1998 NBA Finals, or Simone Biles, a USA women's gymnast considered the greatest of all time. These athletes are calm under pressure. Consider baseball and softball players: they approach game-changing moments (last up at bat) with the same calmness as they do the game's first pitch. They know that anxiety, stress, and frustration while trailing in points won't help them perform better; however, remaining calm will.

These ballplayers don't swing faster, slower, or more erratically in given situations. They choose their pitch and swing at the same forceful tempo in every game, all seasons. They can do this because their heart rate and breathing remain steady in a state of calmness, allowing them to maintain their focus and control. Participating in regular-season games or being the state champions will be the same for them. They understand their performance during the regular season brought them to the championship. Being calm during the regular season should carry over into the championship if they want the same result: winning. Being overly anxious because of the venue will not make a player better.

You can adopt these effective strategies to tackle many challenges in your life. As mentioned earlier, staying calm can be beneficial in disagreements with others or unexpected daily events. It's crucial to note that the obstacles you face need not be monumental or life-threatening to justify the development and execution of a thoughtful plan. Even everyday situations, such as a demanding work project or interpersonal conflicts, can lead to significant stress and anxiety. By applying a structured approach to these seemingly minor issues, you can cultivate resilience, enhance your problem-solving skills, and ultimately improve your overall well-being.

In summary, it's crucial to cultivate calmness, assess the situation, and develop a plan to address challenges effectively. If you emphasize one of the steps expressed here, it would be to remain calm. Take a moment to pause, breathe deeply, and center yourself before diving into problem-solving. Your practice of remaining calm allows you to think more clearly and creatively about your options. Lastly, the sooner you begin formulating and executing a meaningful plan, the more swiftly you can progress through your situation.

Chapter 6
You Never Know

Going into the unknown is how you expand what is known.
— **Abby St. Jacques**

There is a lot of negativities in how people treat others. But not to be completely cynical, there is a lot of good in the world by those who go out of their way to help and support others in their time of need. I encourage you to keep your eye out for both. Noticing the negativity will help you avoid spending too much time around it and seeing the positivity will help you gravitate toward it. This increased awareness of both will enlighten you about how others around you operate and how you want to live your life.

While you go about your daily life—whether at work, school, with friends, or running errands—pay attention to those who show kindness to others. A display of kind gestures, such as holding a door open for someone who could use it or helping with a project without being asked, encourages goodwill. At the same time, remain aware of those who exhibit harmful behaviors, such as spreading rumors or undermining others' efforts. Recognizing these negative behaviors can empower you to support those affected by negativity.

Always remember that the power of positivity resides within you, ready to be expressed and shared with the world. Conversely, the negativity that others may display—

whether through criticism, frustration, or unkind words—does not have to be taken to heart or become a reflection of your self-worth. By focusing on your inner strength and maintaining an optimistic outlook, you can rise above external negativity and cultivate a sense of peace and resilience that empowers you to navigate challenges gracefully. Therefore, embrace your ability to spread positivity and let it shine brightly, regardless of the circumstances around you and how others may display their negativity.

Just because you are surrounded by people with negative attitudes and destructive behaviors does not mean you have to emulate or engage in their actions. Your boundaries are your shield, giving you the power and authority to protect yourself from their negativity. Do not let their actions breach your boundaries and influence you to participate in what they do. Your limit on what you are willing to accept is within your control. By maintaining your boundaries, you assert your strength and resilience, refusing to let their negativity affect you.

Do not allow anyone to pull you into their routine of hurting others, taking what is not yours, or failing to achieve your best. Following negativity or being emotionally changed by it could drastically change your life. If this happens, you may end up far from where your life could have been had you not become involved or allowed their influence to affect you.

Allowing others to negatively influence you will not improve your life or the lives of those you encounter later.

This is because adverse events reduce the likelihood of positive events, as they have a negative impact. When you become involved with those who create negativity, you may never know how great things could have been in your own life had you stayed on track with your positive, purposeful ambitions.

Therefore, avoid those with negative aims and keep your direction positive and moving forward. Do not become involved with others who only have negative things to say about you. It is most likely because they only have negative comments about themselves. Don't let their comments attach themselves to you or your goals, overshadow your hopes, or take apart your dreams.

You can achieve this by actively recognizing and appreciating the spontaneous acts of kindness you encounter daily, whether from friends, family, or even strangers. Moreover, strive to contribute positively to your well-being—through practices like self-care, gratitude, and encouragement—and to the environment around you, fostering a community where compassion and support thrive. By doing so, you cultivate a culture of kindness that enriches yourself and those you interact with. Doing so makes you emotionally, mentally, and physically invested in yourself and your surroundings. The stronger the bond, the more difficult it will be for negativity from others to penetrate.

Stay strong in who you are. Believe in your abilities and keep working toward your ambitions. Brush aside incoming negativity and work even harder toward your dreams. Your positive mindset is a powerful tool. Believe that you can do anything you set your mind on. Embrace unexpected adverse events in life and respond positively to disappointment. Turn your disappointments into something positive. Often, it is through disappointment that people can maximize their potential. Remember, adversity can catalyze growth and serve as a stepping stone to success.

Keep in mind that both the positivity and negativity of others have shaped your path leading up to today. The uplifting words of those who believe in you have propelled you forward, while the critical comments of those who doubt you have fueled your determination. Therefore, recognize that encouragement from your well-wishers can be as inspiring as criticism from your detractors. Both positive and negative experiences can transform the moments in our lives into opportunities for growth and motivation. Draw inspiration from both positive and negative events, which can serve as stepping-stones to greater gains.

Let me share an example. I was driving on a fast-paced highway when someone abruptly cut in front of me. It was frustrating, as I had to slow down quickly and change lanes to avoid being too close to their rear bumper. The driver who cut in front of me significantly altered my driving experience, forcing me to distance myself from other cars to avoid a potential accident. This aggressive behavior by another driver allows me to share this principle of positives, negatives, and 'you never know.'

Many drivers, put in my position, would see this as a negative situation or a disappointment in their driving experience. I view them as a blessing. This is because good things can come from adverse events. When such events happen, you never know the outcome until later. Often, situations that seem negative on the surface turn out to be positive. Conversely, situations that seem positive on the surface turn into negatives. In this case, a negative turned into a positive. Because I moved to an adjacent lane, I could now see the line of cars I just moved out of.

Up ahead, the cars were slowing down abruptly, some skidding to a stop to avoid colliding with the ones in front of them. The potential danger was evident, and I was grateful for the unexpected opportunity to avoid being entangled in it. Hence, it's all about perspective. I placed myself in a safer position by seeing the situation as an opportunity rather than a setback, and by moving to the adjacent lane rather than honking and remaining behind the person who cut in front of me. I turned a potentially harmful event into a positive outcome.

If I had become upset with the driver who cut in front of me, I might have tailgated them to show my anger. This would have made me look like a fool later if my car had become like the other cars, quickly breaking to a stop. Therefore, you can see that you never know the outcomes of events. Events you are pushed into, and think might have adverse effects, can turn out fine, while events you remain stubborn to leave, assuming you have an advantage, can turn out less than you expected. I turned the negative experience into a positive outcome by going with the flow and not escalating the event.

Events like this happen to everyone all the time in many different forms. I used an example of me being cut off by another vehicle, but similar events occur at the supermarket, like someone taking your place in line or grabbing the last item on a shelf right before you reach for it. The lesson here is: don't be upset when you experience adverse events. You never know how life will turn out after being inconvenienced. You might be in a better situation after the adverse event. Therefore, there is no need to retaliate or plan a quick, vengeful attack when someone has wronged you.

Don't feel compelled to lower your standards of kindness toward others at that moment when someone has taken liberties against you. You might come out ahead due to their negativity. Instead, be resilient in the moment and not let seemingly adverse events bring you down. It might be reassuring to realize that most negative interactions between people fade away and are often overlooked if we don't dwell on the actions or attitudes involved. Therefore, let things pass by you more quickly and see how they turn out over time.

In contrast, when physical gestures or verbal opinions are expressed during a hostile altercation, the emotions tied to those actions persist. The negativity of gestures and hurtful words can replay in a person's mind on a loop. Consequently, the feelings each person experiences due to these actions will linger far longer than the conflict itself. As a result, it becomes challenging for individuals to let go of how they feel after such situations. The feelings and emotions attributed to actions often last longer and cut deeper than the actions themselves.

While the memories of disruptive actions may fade, the emotions stirred up by the event will persist long after. The clarity of recalling actions will be less specific than the genuine emotions experienced by both parties after an event. In other words, recalling who did what, to whom, and how will be more challenging than expressing the feelings both could share about the event.

You have heard the phrase, 'Words cut like a knife.' Well, it is true. Additionally, wounds caused by comments and actions take longer to heal than the events that caused them. Managing anger, aggression, and actions is essential because they are rarely forgotten once expressed.

Another reason to avoid anger and aggression is because they often hit their mark. People know how to hurt each other with their words and actions. If you communicate your anger and frustration to others, you cannot retract them. What is done is done. Therefore, be careful what you say, why, how, and when. Keeping your emotions in check is the best way to prevent lasting pain, since the outcomes of situations can be unpredictable.

Suppose you express your anger the moment you feel it. In that case, you may later realize that you are in a better position because of their actions, making you look foolish for confronting them. As mentioned earlier, adverse outcomes might turn in your favor, just as potential positives may sour. Therefore, keep in mind that controlling your emotions is a decisive step toward feeling less vulnerable.

Think of it in this light: tomorrow's events are inherently unpredictable. Consequently, we cannot erase the negative emotions expressed during a regretful incident. Therefore, the key is to allow the disappointment to run its course while you gather yourself. If you're upset about how something unfolded, take a moment to be patient and observe how things progress.

If you need to express your disappointment about an incident, remember it's always wiser to do so in a more controlled environment later than in the heat of the moment. Furthermore, expressing negative feelings in a controlled way later can enhance your maturity level. As a guiding principle, expressing negative emotions at the moment rarely yields positive results. This is because there hasn't been time for events to find their prospective place. Once things settle, it will be much easier to discuss events calmly and logically.

As the saying goes, 'Hindsight is 20/20,' meaning we clearly understand events once they've passed. Therefore, we must restrain our frustration with every trial, as we can't predict the future. Being frustrated today about an event that may resolve itself tomorrow wastes our energy. We must accept what comes our way, knowing we did our best in that moment. While we can't predict or control the future, we can control our actions, and that's a decisive step in the right direction toward forming a better, more predictable life.

Don't let adverse events distract you from your goals, hopes, and dreams. If you let them, they will only serve as distractions. Instead, let minor setbacks unfold without much opposition when things don't go your way. Their outcomes may be beneficial in the long run. Hence, you never know how things will turn out. When one event doesn't align with your plans, it may open doors to new opportunities. By not wasting time on things beyond your control, you'll have more time and energy to focus on what you can change.

Let's revisit the driving scenario, a situation we all might encounter, to illustrate the concept of this chapter, 'You Never Know.' You should be completely aware that I have no control over the driver who cut in front of me. However, I do have control over my actions. Therefore, it's empowering to realize that I can choose not to let my emotions escalate into venting my anger. I choose to keep my emotions and actions to myself because I never know what the result will be. I'd rather not embarrass myself by overreacting if the outcome turns out to be in my favor.

Honking my horn may have made the other driver more aggressive. It may have also given them another reason to retaliate. Additionally, speeding up and closing the gap between my vehicle and the one ahead of me to prevent the other vehicle from cutting between us would have put my vehicle in a worse position, as the cars were about to stop abruptly. Therefore, it was best I did nothing. By 'doing nothing,' I mean not reacting impulsively or aggressively. Sometimes, it is better to stay calm and see how the situation unfolds than make a hasty decision that could worsen it.

It will always benefit you to look for the positive aspects of a negative situation. This approach equips you with a powerful tool to navigate the challenges life throws your way. By finding the silver lining in the darkest clouds, you equip yourself to tackle and conquer the difficulties that may otherwise seem insurmountable. By focusing on the positive, you'll see opportunities where others see roadblocks. Therefore, remember there's no benefit in allowing frustration, anger, or prolonged negativity to take hold when faced with unexpected circumstances.

Expressing frustration with yourself and others will only lead you in circles. Circles are closed loops that do not have a beginning or ending point. Being frustrated about something that has happened should be only a quick springboard to finding a solution. If you remain frustrated, you will do nothing to solve the problem, like circles that do not advance; they only move within the same path.

Consequently, after some expended energy, you will end up at the point where the problem began. Therefore, the quicker you get past being upset, the faster you can continue living your life. What should be noted is that 'moving on' doesn't mean forgetting or ignoring the problem. It means accepting the situation, learning from it, and finding a way to grow from it.

I can confidently tell you that in-the-moment responses to things that have upset you do not turn out well. This is because when you are upset, you often project heated responses, full of spontaneous reactions and defense mechanisms. Through my experiences and hearing of others', I have found that things can improve when a person sits back and reflects on what bothers them. If you sit back and think about how to express your anger, two things will come to mind. First, you may have taken better steps to prevent the event from happening. Second, perhaps this outcome is for the best, as one can never predict how situations will unfold.

In my experience, there are no absolutes, meaning there is no final endpoint at which a person must vent their frustrations and become angry. There's always a chance that adverse events will change or improve in the future. Suppose you're feeling frustrated about a project at work. In this case, a new idea or opportunity could surface to turn the situation around. Other examples of not giving in to frustration or being upset include being frustrated by a low exam score or by poor performance in a team sport. In these cases, there's always a chance the same situation will occur again, and you will have an opportunity to redeem yourself. Therefore, never give in to being upset. Things have a way of working out.

Do not give up when faced with opposition, setbacks, or resistance. If you need to change your tactics or alter your path toward your goals, it's okay, but don't give in to opposition. Always strive to keep progressing toward your goals, and whenever you face challenges or setbacks, focus on transforming the negatives into valuable opportunities for growth and improvement. Embrace each obstacle as a chance to learn, adapt, and emerge stronger than before. If you do, you will find, more often than not, terrible situations are not so bad, and poor situations get better. Letting the events continue their path works to your advantage. In hindsight, retaliating against negativity can backfire and make things worse.

Suppose someone is making negative comments to others about you or your work performance, and how you live your life. If you know you are living well, not bothering anyone, and being kind, you have no reason to retaliate. Instead, try these strategies: First, acknowledge the comment without getting defensive. Second, redirect the conversation to a positive aspect of your work or life. Third, if the remarks persist, calmly express your disagreement, or ask for clarification on what they have noticed. These routes reduce negativity and empower you to steer the narrative positively by quickly and carefully shutting down negative comments.

Conversely, engaging with others negatively and retaliating toward them for their negativity will put you in the same negative light as the other person, which is not a better position. In this situation and others like it, rely on the phrase of this chapter, 'You Never Know,' to guide the outcome once you have confronted the issue and moved past it. For instance, suppose a supervisor overhears these things about you and investigates to find the comments are unfounded, setting the other person straight. Because of this, you come out looking great. However, if you retaliate by saying negative things about them, you are also wrong, and both will be set straight by supervisors.

The best response is not to get caught up in the negative actions of others who want to cheat, lie, and steal. Let them run their course of falling into trouble. Those who cause trouble are more likely to fall into poor circumstances. Knowing this, stay clear of them. Instead of being bothered by their actions, focus on the positive aspects of your journey. Maintain focus on your goals and continue moving forward as best you can. The more you let others' actions upset you, the more time they take away from your journey.

However, it may be challenging to distance yourself from people who negatively impact your well-being. Consequently, it may be challenging to maintain the 'you never know' perspective when dealing with negativity. Perhaps others have won a couple of battles to get you to participate in their negativity. By winning a couple of battles, these individuals can easily distract you from your self-improvement efforts and may have succeeded in dampening your ambitions. Circumstances like these typically emerge when you indulge in behaviors that aren't beneficial or when their negativity dampens your drive to better your situation.

When you feel things are not going your way and those around you are trying to bring you down while you are trying to improve yourself, tell yourself, "It is not over until it is over." This phrase helps empower the mind and body during many situations, particularly when playing sports. Compare your ambitions to what you want as an athlete would when they're focusing on winning. If you're trailing in points or falling behind in a race, keep pushing until the whistle blows or the final second ticks away. Now, if you've lost a competition or missed a goal, try to strengthen your inner motivation. Convince yourself that the competition isn't truly over. Even if the event has concluded for everyone else, remind yourself that it continues for you. Start setting up to win the next competition or achieve your previously missed goal.

Others may have turned your focus toward their negativity, but that does not mean you must dwell on it. Remember, things work out best when you stay the course and keep moving forward with your best efforts toward seeing everything as positive. Keep your established patterns intact by not letting others' negativity take hold of your positive patterns. Tell yourself things are not over until it's over. Your positive outlook on your goals is what keeps things alive.

You can continue to struggle and come out on top by working toward the next competition. You can begin to prepare for the next race, next game, or next ambition as soon as the whistle sounds for the one you just lost. You may not have done well in the competition or in your objectives that just ended, but you can still work toward them again. Therefore, keep in mind that it's never over, even if you think it looks that way. If you do not allow adverse events to discourage you, you can use them as a learning opportunity to keep striving for your desired goal until you achieve it. Keep moving forward; you never know what will happen.

Sometimes, when you are a part of a competition, the winner collects the first-place award only to find out they are disqualified for one reason or another, and the prize goes to the second-place finisher. If you had competed against this person, not given up, and taken second place, you would now be the winner, as the first-place person was disqualified. You never know how things will turn out, so keep pushing forward in all that you do. While watching competitive sports, I've noticed many times when the person in the lead lets their guard down because they become too confident. This complacency can open the door for someone trailing behind to slip past and claim first place. Therefore, using the example above, don't lose hope in what you're striving for if others are ahead of you and you lack confidence, just keep pushing forward and finish. You never know how things will turn out.

Let me share one last story with you. The message helped me understand the concept of 'you never know.' A farmer and his son enjoyed their lives on a small ranch. The son was responsible for their young horse. The horse was well cared for and helped the family earn a living by pulling a plow in their fields. One summer day, the horse ran away. A neighbor noticed the horse was not around and approached the farmer to say, "I see your horse ran away; that is terrible!" The farmer replied, "Maybe so, maybe not, you never know."

A few more days passed, and their horse returned. Following their horse home and into the barn were a few wild stallions. The farmer and his son now had several beautiful horses – his original horse and his new ones. The neighbors noticed one day and shouted, "I see your horse has returned and brought several other horses. That is wonderful!" The farmer replied, "Maybe so, maybe not. You never know."

Later that same week, the farmer's son climbed onto a wild horse to ride it, but it bucked him off, breaking the boy's leg. The neighbors, watching this event, shouted, "Looks like your son broke his leg; that is terrible!" The farmer replied, "Maybe so, maybe not. You never know." As timing would have it, military soldiers marched through town a week later, gathering all physically able young men to join the front lines and fight. The soldiers did not take the farmer's son because of his broken leg. The neighbors shouted, "Your son was spared from the fighting; that is wonderful!" The farmer replied, "Maybe so, maybe not. We'll see."

As the story shows, it is impossible to predict how life's events will turn out. Numerous unaccounted-for variables exist for every action, making life a fascinating journey of unpredictability. Initial reactions to situations may be happy or sad, but unpredictable factors can turn positive moments into sad ones and negative moments into happy ones. You never truly know the consequences of misfortune or good fortune. In any situation, things may seem wonderful at first, but become disappointing within a short time. Similarly, you may be disappointed by a problem at first, but within a short time, events might turn out to be what you've hoped for.

It is important to recognize that change is the only constant in our universe. Everything is constantly changing, evolving in ways we might not always notice. Consequently, there is little justification for labeling a situation as hopelessly terrible or entirely wonderful. With the change of time and unknown variables, terrible can become wonderful, and wonderful can turn terrible. The reality we experience is often a mere facade, masking deeper truths beneath the surface.

Life unfolds as a complex tapestry of events, where some align with our desires and aspirations while others seem to thwart them. Everything that happens in life is just a series of events. Some events go your way, and others do not. Understanding this, a question arises: who can truly determine whether circumstances are favorable or unfavorable when their impact is subject to personal interpretation? In other words, who is to say if you believe things are going your way when they appear not to be?

In the grand scheme of existence, our perceptions of events are often fleeting and can shift dramatically over time and with perspective. Therefore, it is crucial to approach each situation with an open mind, recognizing that every experience, whether positive or negative, contributes to our growth and understanding. In the grand scheme of things, positive events can have an adverse impact on your life, while negative events can have a favorable effect. Because life is always unpredictable and change is bound to happen randomly, you never know the outcome of events in anyone's life.

If you choose to believe everything is going your way, it will only be a matter of time before things do. And in all fairness, even when things are not going your way, they will eventually. Continue looking for the best possible position to put yourself in when things do not go your way. Continue maintaining your positive mindset, even if all appears lost, or others have stolen your thunder.

Furthermore, make the best possible move in all the poor positions you are dealt. This outlook on life can give you a significant advantage in creating a life where the outcomes are shaped by the idea that 'you never know.'

Critical Thinking and Courage

Concepts of courage and critical thinking are typically seen as unrelated. Courage is often defined as bravery, usually experienced in spontaneous moments. In contrast, critical thinking involves logic and systematic reasoning, emerging from careful contemplation. However, these two qualities have a common foundation: both require a willingness to confront the unknown. Courage manifests in physical actions, while critical thinking is reflected in cognitive efforts.

Courage, often an unexpected visitor, emerges in moments that catch a person off guard. This type of courage is not a planned response but a spontaneous reaction to unforeseen situations. It represents the readiness to confront uncertainty, which is frequently associated with danger, though not exclusively. Courage is the ability to tackle challenges posed by overwhelming, unknown circumstances, and critical thinking is essential to nurturing this willingness to face the unfamiliar.

For instance, an individual might critically assess the potential risks and benefits of standing up for a colleague in a challenging situation. Engaging in this critical thinking process enables a person to make a more informed, strategic decision about their courageous actions. Therefore, it is clear that critical thinking requires time to develop fully, allowing conflicting thoughts to surface. Furthermore, this process is not limited to a single perspective; rather, it enables competing viewpoints to be considered equally important until their merit is validated or disproven.

When we shift our focus to critical thinking, it becomes clear that it unfolds in a logical sequence. Each step is carefully taken, leading us to a conclusion rooted in solid reasoning and deep understanding. This progression contrasts sharply with the concept of courage, in which actions demonstrating bravery often occur spontaneously. However, there are instances when the decision to step forward in bravery regarding a situation has been carefully considered over time. In these moments, courage and critical thinking intersect, fostering a sense of self-improvement that enhances self-awareness and consciousness regarding a person's actions.

As mentioned earlier, critical thinking and courage share common ground. For instance, embracing the unknown through critical thinking enables those who initially lack courage to discover it while implementing a brave act. This being noted, the process of critical thinking requires bravery to stand up for oneself and others who cannot. Additionally, it's important to recognize the courage it takes to come forward after carefully considering the complete picture of events. After reviewing the full account of any event, one may find oneself at a loss about its outcome; therefore, assuming responsibility for it takes courage.

At any rate, both views described above are courageous. The first acted and built critical thinking around their bravery; the second needed time to think critically about their involvement before acting bravely by coming forward. In both cases, courage is not just a result of critical thinking; it is also a necessary component of it, as it takes courage to confront the unknown and challenge the status quo.

Some might say critical thinking after a courageous event is an instrument for evaluating its consequences, learning from experiences, and making better decisions in the future. Thus, this reflective process makes us more responsible for our actions as we understand the impact of our choices. For instance, a person might critically evaluate a situation and realize that the standard practice is unjust or ineffective.

This realization, fueled by critical thinking, inspires and motivates one to come forward and propose a change, even if it means challenging the status quo. An example might be advocating for a more inclusive workplace policy or challenging a discriminatory practice. Another example could be a student who critically evaluates a teacher's unfair grading policy and then courageously speaks up to propose a more equitable system.

The previous examples testify to the transformative power of critical thinking. It can change a person's perspective, giving them the courage to stand up for what is right and challenge the status quo. By questioning the validity of habitual actions, critical thinking helps one understand that longevity does not make every past event correct. Consequently, doing the right thing is a sign of courage, especially when a standard of doing the wrong thing has been in place for a while. Hence, the transformative power of critical thinking can and should inspire and motivate us to act courageously in the face of adversity.

Those who practice critical thinking act courageously, doing what is sound, just, and proper, even when it opposes habitual actions. It should also be noted that it takes courage to think critically about prior actions and adjust them to align with the proper process. Therefore, it is understandable that saying something has been performed consistently or in a particular fashion does not make it right.

When applied correctly, critical thinking assesses each repetitive event as unique without assuming that subsequent events must mirror the previous one. The idea that comes to mind is, 'Just because something happened twice doesn't mean the first instance was right.' Critical thinking challenges this flawed logic, courageously shedding light on the situation.

Thinking critically (or purposeful reflection) can help us question the validity of habitual actions and understand that just because something has been done a certain way for a long time doesn't mean it's the best way. This approach empowers you to speak up about issues and irregularities when things need to be reviewed and changed from their consistent patterns. It instills confidence in questioning and challenging the status quo and the unknown, and it allows us to be courageous enough to actively engage in the change process.

What is your definition of *courage*? Write it down so you can revisit and reflect on it.

How is *courage* tied to critical thinking?

How has your *courage* (or lack of) impacted your life up to this point?

How do critical thinking skills strengthen a person's sense of *courage*?

Explain how developing a progressive sense of *courage* can positively impact a person's life.

Explain how the absence of developing a sense of *courage* may hurt a person's life. (For instance, avoiding potential dangers, understanding personal emotions, etc.)

Express how you feel about *courage* being one of the most essential things in a successful life. (You may need to define the term successful.)

Chapter 7
Continual Resistance

Beware the quiet man. For while others speak, he watched. And while others act, he plans. And when they finally rest... he strikes.

— **Anonymous**

When we look at the human body, we witness an incredible system that reacts to every push and pull of resistance. This resistance is key in strengthening our physical muscles, minds, and emotions. As we build our strength, our bodies can handle even greater challenges. This systematic and gradual process of resistance training enhances our strength and stamina, instilling a profound sense of full-body empowerment. Thus, gaining strength not only affects our skeletal muscles but also our brains. While the brain isn't categorized as a muscle, it similarly responds positively to increased challenges, especially after being fortified through resistance.

The brain functions similarly to muscles, with its complex cellular structure playing a key role in its strength. It grows mentally stronger with regular use and becomes more adaptable when faced with challenges, even in stressful or anxious situations. This remarkable responsiveness highlights the brain's resilience and ability to overcome obstacles. Through consistent practice, the brain strengthens and adapts to its surroundings. The secret to this adaptability lies in facing continuous challenges, often from the learning process. As we tackle mental, emotional, and psychological hurdles that once seemed daunting, the brain demonstrates its incredible capacity to adapt, process, and analyze information effectively.

At my high school gym, a sign hangs above the door leading from the locker room to the weight room. It reads, "The tested can always take it." This message is a powerful reminder that testing is crucial in identifying and measuring an item's strength, durability, and composition. It also allows us to evaluate the quality and reliability of what is being tested. When we push our muscles, we lift heavier weights or do more repetitions, gradually building strength and endurance. This concept also extends to our brains through overcoming academic challenges, difficult relationships, and overwhelming projects, among other things. Dealing with these life situations reinforces what we've learned, increases our knowledge base, and strengthens our brains to perform resiliently the next time they occur.

We increase our brain power by testing our experiences' and acquired knowledge's limits and boundaries. Repetitive assessments of a person's knowledge will improve and strengthen their understanding and awareness of the material they have processed. Assessments will also identify areas that need improvement. Testing and evaluating are vital to any process to maintain growth and progress. Consequently, there are significant measures to gauge progress, including weightlifting to build muscle strength and conducting assessments to improve mental resilience.

When building muscle, it's crucial to periodically add heavier weights or other forms of resistance, such as more reps, to continually build stronger muscles. Muscle growth will plateau if you stick with the same weight from start to finish of your year-long workout plan, without increasing the weight or the number of repetitions. A growing young adult like yourself will outgrow your ability to lift that initial amount as you get older and stronger. Lifting that same weight over the years may keep the muscle active, which is good, but it will not support an increase in size to handle more challenging loads. Using the term 'load,' I am referring to events and situations in life that create a struggle. And as you can tell by now, the term 'weight' refers to similar events in life that cause a burden or struggle.

Similarly, for the brain, a person must constantly gather new knowledge and periodically assess it to build brain power. If no new information is collected and processed during the brain's development journey, it will not continue to be strengthened to handle more challenging events. The brain needs continuous challenges to grow cognitively stronger. It's unrealistic to think reading a first-grade-level book during childhood and continuing it into adulthood will lead to greater knowledge, mental strength, and improved reading ability. You will outgrow your ability to read these first-grade-level books and process the information in them as you grow older, interact with others, and work through life's experiences. However, with progressive resistance (reading more challenging texts), there is always the potential for growth and development.

Switching gears but staying on the topic of developing muscles. A place where the body experiences atrophy is in outer space. Atrophy is the term for the process by which the body wastes away. Muscles and other parts of the body degrade and stop growing. Atrophy occurs in space because gravity (a natural resistance to human movement) is much less than on Earth. Astronauts exercise approximately 2 hours each day to compensate for the lack of gravity resistance they would experience on Earth. As a result, the force of gravity on Earth serves as the essential resistance individuals need to build and strengthen their muscles.

Relating this concept to the human brain, reading the same types of picture books you read in early elementary school and taking the same kinds of intellectual assessments you did in elementary school will not improve brain power. Through repetitive reading of the same information at this young age, you will outgrow the resistance experienced in elementary school. Hence, there will be no resistance to your brain if you stay at that level of knowledge as you get older.

Therefore, you must challenge yourself by reading more solid literature like chapter books, novels, and peer-reviewed articles as you move up in years. This progressive learning process is not a suggestion but a necessity for your brain's strength and development, as it can shape intellectual growth. When the brain is challenged with new stimuli to learn, process, and evaluate, it strengthens.

Encouraging the brain to explore new ideas while engaging in reflective thinking is more than just stretching its boundaries; it's a journey toward a richer, more comprehensive perspective. Using academics as an example, you challenge your brain to respond by adding new experiences through reading, course assignments, tasks, responsibilities, and outside-school challenges. These experiences create new opportunities to strengthen your understanding of the world, as you will see it differently from others. Therefore, embrace the challenges and assessments you encounter. They are not set in place to weaken, but to give you strength. Hence, resistance needs to be viewed as a tool for growth.

Continual resistance to cognition is an underrated asset, as we must constantly strengthen our minds. Stronger, better-developed minds lead to fewer poor decisions. As a teacher, I have seen the effect of poor decision-making and how it can affect people. Some poor decisions can trigger a disastrous series of events, including gaslighting—a form of psychological manipulation aimed at instilling doubt in a specific individual. This can lead to heated arguments, the breakdown of friendships, and even worse repercussions.

Often, a person's weak cognitive skills and poor decision-making can unknowingly lead another person down a destructive path of wrongdoing. In the grand scheme of things, some decisions may destroy a business or partnership and even bring countries to the brink of war. Since all decisions arise from the power and discipline of the brain, it is imperative to strengthen the brain through the resistance offered by progressively challenging experiences. Continual challenges will boost your cognitive abilities, leading to better decision-making.

Most poor decisions could be avoided if the person making the decision had a more thorough understanding of the variables involved in their situation. This is because a more versatile outlook stems from viewing situations from various angles, and gaining these different perspectives is essential for a comprehensive understanding. Consequently, the ability to form different perspectives comes from 'brain power,' developed through continual and progressive resistance.

Resistance to enhancing cognitive abilities can manifest in various ways. It may involve overcoming procrastination by implementing effective time management strategies, such as setting specific goals and creating structured schedules. Additionally, challenging oneself to learn new skills or acquire knowledge through formal education, self-study, or engaging in stimulating discussions plays a crucial role in mental development. Moreover, tackling complex tasks—breaking them down into manageable steps and maintaining a persistent attitude despite difficulties—can significantly improve overall 'brain power.' By consciously pushing against these resistances, individuals can unlock their potential for intellectual growth and adaptability.

You can strengthen your mind daily by engaging in your secondary and formal education, pushing yourself to be a better athlete and teammate, and deepening your meaningful relationships, etc. These areas of life, and many more like them, strengthen your brain through challenging events. The only drawback is it will take time. It will not happen overnight. But it will happen. Give yourself the chance to strengthen your mind by getting more involved in positive, productive activities around you, such as those mentioned above. Additionally, you will benefit from your efforts to boost your brainpower, including improved memory, problem-solving skills, and decision-making abilities.

Conversely, a person with weak mental ability will have difficulty excelling in the areas above. They will also have difficulty avoiding arguments, staying out of trouble, and building a path toward progress. A person with weak cognitive ability will have trouble saying 'no' to things they should say 'no' to. Saying 'no' to illegal things takes brain power, as does saying 'no' to participating in destructive activities such as violence, bullying, vandalism, and graffiti.

Those participating in these activities see only the event itself, not the cause and effect. They do not have the mental capacity to comprehend the destruction they cause themselves and others. Therefore, I encourage you to build your cognitive abilities (brainpower) as you grow and learn as a young adult. Challenge yourself with activities that require mental effort, such as science courses, team sports, and orchestra (band). By their very nature, these activities require a person to push their mental limits, strengthening brain power.

Strengthening your brain power is all about challenging yourself and staying within the environments that allow you to think critically. If you are part of the orchestra (or band), on a team sport, or taking an honors course, stay in them until the season ends or the course finishes. These environments are designed to push your mental boundaries and foster critical thinking. If it is challenging to be in school, stay in the challenge until you graduate. If you are in a career you enjoy, keep reading about your job details and learning more about your career. If you are not in any of these, I suggest you hang around others who will challenge you.

Have you heard the saying, "Iron sharpens iron"? This phrase is a metaphor illustrating how experiencing challenging events alongside people who are also pushing themselves through similar ones can strengthen us. Essentially, you need to be exposed to strong, resilient experiences to become stronger and more resilient. Consequently, to truly achieve strength, it's essential to immerse yourself in the presence of stronger and more challenging things. Therefore, embrace challenges and resistance; it will make you stronger. Connecting this concept to our life experiences, it's tough to grow and expand your imagination if you keep returning to the same book you've already memorized. Like progressing from elementary school, learning requires stepping out of our comfort zone and exploring new academic, social, or work-related narratives.

If you are not experiencing challenges or resistance to improvement, do something about it. 'Find a new book.' Find a better job. Find more challenging athletic activities. Find more friends if your existing ones aren't challenging you to grow. You don't have to leave the old ones; just find new ones to challenge you. Find ways to implement continual resistance; it will make you stronger. It is impossible not to grow from resistance and being challenged.

By the nature of the journey, you will change due to your efforts to struggle. When you are engaged in these struggles of change, remember that the struggle is objective and what leads you to be a better person. The actual destination will not change you, but the events along the way will. Therefore, reflect on the resistance you are engaged in, rather than on the distance you have overcome through your struggles. Everyone experiences events differently, resulting in unique personal changes. To use a metaphor, don't worry much about the length of the race or the finish line; focus on incorporating resistance along the way. Whether you cross the finish line or not, you will gain strength from the resistance.

Racing against others can sometimes be discouraging because people compare themselves to others with different advantages and resources. It is unfair to anyone to put that kind of pressure on themselves. Instead, people should look for the PRs (personal records). Therefore, enjoy the process of life; it is more important than the race through life. If you let the process of resistance work and ignore being in a race as a competition with others, you will reach the same destination. On top of this, resistance does not care about other people you compare yourself to. Furthermore, resistance should be connected to your personal experiences to create a meaningful sense of struggle from which you can grow and improve.

Your level of resistance has nothing to do with other people. Resistance should be a part of your life for your benefit, not for the benefit of others. In other words, gaining strength through resistance is a process, not a race. In the next book in this series, Part 4, there is a chapter titled " It's a Process, not a Race, " which explains that a person cannot expect to achieve a year's worth of growth by consuming an entire year's worth of food in a single meal. It is impossible. The body needs time to process the food, draw energy from it, and gradually develop growth over the years. Similarly, the brain must process information to grow and strengthen. Therefore, your resistance needs to be tailored to your experiences and abilities and not a standard others use.

When we relate resistance and growth, we see that acquiring information might be a daily activity, but gaining knowledge, understanding, and wisdom takes time. It is a process of continually gathering, assimilating, and reflecting on information, leading to understanding and, eventually, wisdom. For instance, cramming for an assessment the night before will not have a lasting effect on learning. Facts and concepts might be gained through cramming, but the understanding, wisdom, and usefulness of that information have yet to develop. Its application will be short-lived because it has little ability to retain information.

Furthermore, cramming a large amount of information into your brain quickly is not an effective way to gain a lasting understanding or develop wisdom. The brain's short-term memory is not designed to retain information for future reflection. Instead, aim for gradual learning over weeks and months for lasting results. Deep understanding and wisdom about specific topics often take years to develop. The time invested in gathering and processing information is the essential 'resistance' required to foster understanding and cultivate wisdom. Resistance is what the brain needs to grow stronger. By allowing the brain to absorb information slowly over time, you're allowing yourself to grow through continual resistance.

Cramming information into your brain quickly will not develop understanding or wisdom. It will produce a lot of information in your brain, but it will fade in a day or two, maybe even within a few hours. Therefore, it is easy to see that actual progress is not made by cramming things together in life but by continual resistance, which refers to the deliberate effort to slow down, reflect, and apply acquired knowledge. Moments of reflection and pauses to consider their connection to prior knowledge ideally deepen understanding and lead to wisdom.

Take your time in the process of personal development. Do this by learning today what is required of you in your academic journey, in your career, or in your friendships. Slowly build upon what you know and accept that it takes time and patience to master things. Rushing through assignments, work projects, and relationships will not lead to a better understanding of them. Taking shortcuts with work projects will not produce meaningful accomplishments. Jumping into a relationship without knowing much about the other person will not increase the chances of a lasting friendship.

As you dedicate yourself to all aspects of your life, allow things to progress slowly and methodically. This approach will enable you to build resilience through the challenges you face and gain valuable insights from the obstacles you encounter. In this light, resistance is the foundation that will bolster your growth in education, career, relationships, hobbies, and whatever you decide to take on.

When we compare the resistance and growth of young adults to mature professionals, it becomes clear that successful professionals learn valuable lessons from their mistakes before moving forward. Meanwhile, bright students take the time to absorb new information, ensuring they don't overwhelm themselves with excessive workloads. Consequently, successful professionals learn from a failed project and apply those lessons to future endeavors, as bright students learn from poorly taken quizzes and tests and apply that knowledge to later exams. Taking the comparison a step further, successful professionals use feedback to improve their leadership, as bright students address and learn from material they missed to avoid failing again.

When we compare the resistance and growth of bright students and successful professionals to personal relationships, it is evident that the genuine value of strong and stable relationships develops over time and with purposeful effort rather than haphazardly and quickly. Building meaningful connections requires patience as experiences unfold in both individuals' lives. Sharing life's ups and downs, the good and the bad, takes time. Each person must demonstrate their commitment to 'being there' for the other. As illustrated, the abovementioned situations exemplify the resilience needed to foster significant and enduring relationships.

Let's explore the concept of resistance and its role in knowledge and understanding on a deeper level. To do this, we must first acknowledge that understanding something differs from knowing it. Understanding brings a higher level of awareness, while knowing is more superficial. Consequently, a proper understanding of knowledge develops over time, unlike informational knowledge, which can be gathered quickly. Hence, understanding is the application of resistance in learning.

Let's explore the concept of resistance and its role in a deeper understanding and assessed wisdom. To do this, we must first acknowledge that understanding something differs from wisdom. In its simplest form, understanding is developed knowledge, while wisdom is the application of understanding. Unlike simplistic gathered knowledge, understanding, and wisdom should be viewed as a process that involves continual effort, application, and reflection rather than a race to accumulate such information.

Engaging in the process of resistance to application and reflection gives us valuable insights into the efforts and struggles involved. Furthermore, those who claim to 'understand' without applying their knowledge fail to grasp the full depth of true understanding. No one can share 'understanding' without having worked with their knowledge. Knowledge is only information until it is developed into understanding. As a result, people can only share their understanding with others once they have navigated their challenges and reflected on how they have applied what they know.

Let me share a story about cramming for knowledge and losing out on 'understanding.' When I was in high school, my World History teacher had this saying, "If you can't say it, you don't understand it." I remember a time in that class when an individually assigned project was to recite a piece of memorized literature. As the week ended, I quickly picked a piece of literature and began to cram for my presentation. I crammed all night to memorize that piece of literature. The next day, when it was my turn, I stood before the class and began reciting.

About halfway through, I stopped because I couldn't remember anymore. At that point, I realized that 'knowing' differs from 'understanding.' I knew of the literature because I worked with it all night, but did not understand it. If given some more time, I could stumble through it. However, in hindsight, what I needed was to grasp the meaning of the literature so I could recite it smoothly without stumbling or hesitating.

Understanding develops over time as a learner experiences their resistance levels. The piece of literature I chose may have made more sense with more time to work with it. I could have memorized the piece better through logic and reasoning if I had given myself more time. Consequently, there was no continual resistance on my part to engage with the assignment, as I only gave myself a few hours to work on it. If you grasp only one thing from this chapter, let it be this: it is only through continual and progressive resistance that anyone grows stronger and more insightful.

Chapter 8
Knowledge Today is Money Tomorrow

Nothing that is worth anything comes easy.

—**Douglas Allan Portello**

It's often said that knowledge is power, and for good reason. Those who possess knowledge can influence others and shape outcomes to their advantage. This leverage allows individuals to make a meaningful impact. The benefits come from a deep understanding of how things operate, giving knowledgeable people a distinct advantage. When discussing education and knowledge, it's important to recognize that it's not just an academic endeavor but a transformative journey that unlocks potential and establishes the foundation for a successful career. The inspiring impact of an educational journey cannot be overstated, as employers often offer attractive compensation to well-informed candidates.

Large industries pay executives large salaries for their ability to lead others, guide corporations into a solid financial position, and thus become more successful. But it's not only their direct knowledge that earns these positions and salaries; it's the understanding of what their knowledge can do and where to use it. Throughout their career journeys, they have traditionally drawn valuable insights from their past jobs and the experiences of those around them. This enables them to effectively utilize and retain their accumulated knowledge for future opportunities.

Knowledge retention refers to the ability to remember and apply knowledge acquired over time. Moreover, the primary intent behind the concept of knowledge is not so much about gaining it to stockpile, but about using it effectively. Merely accumulating knowledge will keep it as information only. However, applying knowledge will turn it into proper understanding and wealth.

Therefore, in this context, knowledge and income are interconnected; what you know today and are willing to build upon can influence your earnings tomorrow. Thus, developing your knowledge is as important as how you use it to shape your career path. Being a young adult gives you a significant advantage that older people often don't have: you have plenty of time to learn and gain understanding.

Every successful professional had to start somewhere, learning the fundamentals of their trade. They built their knowledge step by step, just like everyone else. With that in mind, it's important to see yourself as no different from their humble beginnings. You are just like they were. Corporate leaders amassed information as they climbed the ranks in their careers and now enjoy substantial salaries. Similarly, as young adults, you gain insight from your surroundings, whether through academic pursuits or your first job. The knowledge you're gaining today sets you up for a well-deserved payoff tomorrow.

Here is a crucial point of this entire chapter. If you don't care about your required secondary education as a young adult or do not take your formal education afterward seriously, why would any employer hire you? They won't. They will likely choose the person who sat beside you, someone who was genuinely invested in what they were learning and who truly cared about their future. Those who approach their studies and work projects with dedication will see their grades and performance evaluations reflect their hard work and commitment. As a result, employers will be more inclined to hire them.

Therefore, start valuing yourself. Dedicate the time and effort necessary to do well in your assignments and excel in them. For example, set aside a specific time each day for studying, ask questions in class, and seek additional resources to deepen your understanding. Your educational efforts are an excellent preparation for even higher education, such as college and trade school. Recognizing the value of your efforts puts you in the driver's seat of your future. Furthermore, college will be significantly more rewarding when you begin to appreciate the importance of your high school effort.

Start valuing yourself. Dedicate the time and effort necessary to do well at work and become invested in what you do. For example, make a conscious commitment to prioritize your tasks, develop a solid work ethic, and continuously seek opportunities for improvement. Your efforts are a perfect preparation for even higher positions, such as management and leadership. Recognizing their value puts you in the driver's seat of your future. Furthermore, higher positions will be significantly more rewarding when you begin to appreciate the importance of the knowledge base you have acquired.

You are in charge of valuing the importance of your time, the efforts you invest, and where you choose to dedicate your energy. However, the consequences will become clear if you put forth only minimal effort and overlook how your education can shape your future and the role your current job plays in your professional growth. I can guarantee that hiring employers will not take you seriously. Why should they? They won't, as there will be plenty of others vying for attention who are willing to put in the hard work to succeed. Remember, learning is the key to a successful future, and it's in your hands to unlock its potential.

Suppose you drift through your education, treating the experience as a casual ride. You put minimal effort into your work, and grades didn't matter much. In this case, the journey afterward will not be as rewarding as if you took it seriously. You will struggle to find a footing in society, secure stable employment, or continue higher education to improve your placement. On the other hand, if you challenge yourself academically to achieve above-average grades, your higher educational experiences and workforce potential will be much more successful.

Considering this, consider your efforts as a 'want to' rather than a 'have to.' The mindset of 'want to' is a powerful motivator that comes from within. It can be cultivated through self-reflection, setting personal goals, and finding passion in what you do. This mindset fuels determination and drives a person to focus on their goals. In this position, very little can stop a person from accomplishing what they set out to achieve.

People who see things as a 'want to' are empowered and driven, achieving more out of life. They are more likely to be hired by companies that are growing successfully and have an educated workforce. On the other hand, those who see things as a 'have to' are less empowered and driven. They view life as drudgery. A person who holds this view will most likely stop doing what is put in front of them at the slightest corrective comment. On the other hand, a person who has a 'want to' work ethic will likely take corrective criticism as a sign to improve what they are working on. In simpler terms, a 'want to' mindset involves doing things for their enjoyment and finding meaning in them, while a 'have to' mindset centers around doing things out of obligation.

For instance, a person with a 'want to' mindset might initiate projects, seek growth opportunities, and strive for excellence in their work. They take on additional responsibilities, volunteer for challenging tasks, and continually seek ways to improve their skills and knowledge. Companies that drive societal change, develop technology, and build societal infrastructure seek people with a 'want to' attitude.

On the other hand, people who see things in terms of 'have to' work on tasks because someone in authority tells them to. People with a 'have to' mindset are hired by companies that provide convenience services, such as fast-food restaurants, movie theaters, and grocery stores. These companies hire individuals who aim to earn a paycheck to meet their daily financial needs.

Switching gears but staying on topic, there are two major hiring categories: those who view life as 'want to' and those who view life as 'have to.' People who excel in their academic education separate themselves from the 'have to' group and become a 'want to.' Therefore, higher education should not be considered only about earning a degree; it's also about shaping your career. It's a catalyst for career growth, telling employers that you are serious about your chosen profession and that you 'want to' be hired to improve their company, not just 'have to' be hired to earn a paycheck.

The 'want to' employees motivate others, while the 'have to' employees must be motivated by others. This is another reason employers prefer 'want to' students as they exit formal education. Therefore, consider all your levels of education as a stepping-stone to becoming a 'want to' employee, which can lead to a brighter future. However, if you currently identify as a 'have to' person in your schooling, take a moment to evaluate your efforts and work on developing habits that will help you transition into a 'want to' person who takes their invested time seriously.

If you decide to invest in yourself through higher education, it's crucial that you take it seriously. Suppose you take it seriously and put in the effort and discipline needed to excel. In that case, this path can significantly improve your job prospects with companies that positively impact society. This being said, there are two main routes to building a successful career. The first involves a straightforward transition from high school to college, where you earn your degree before entering the workforce. The second route offers more flexibility; it lets you jump straight into a job after high school while you work towards your degree.

I took the second path. I worked during the day and went to college in the evening, which took years and was rigorous. Truthfully, no route is better than another, but I wish I had taken the first path. It would have saved me a lot of money and time. I wish I had put more effort into high school, applied for and earned scholarships, transferred directly into college, and then into a career. Unfortunately, I had no one to guide me on the reasons behind these choices.

One of the reasons I wrote these books (a four-part series) is to serve as a guide and narrative mentor, helping young adults understand the importance of making solid, well-informed decisions that have real consequences in shaping their lives. Making good decisions based on good information is a tremendous help in producing a good life. As for me, I finished college with a bachelor's degree at 32. I hope you become highly educated sooner than I did and set out to create a stable future for yourself quicker than I did.

Start motivating yourself today to see the world around you as things you 'want to' do rather than things you 'have to' do. Higher education should be a 'want to.' It's about wanting to finish well, challenge yourself, and strengthen your abilities. Every piece of knowledge you acquire today, this month, and this year is a valuable investment in your future. Once you graduate, businesses will recognize the worth of your efforts. The more skills you develop and the knowledge you gather, the more valuable you become. Think of your education as savings in the bank, promising a high return on investment once you graduate.

Let's consider the same topic from a different angle. Imagine your future employer is hypothetically paying you and several others to be in school and learn as much as possible. When you and the others graduate, the employer will select the best and brightest, as well as those who have dedicated themselves to learning. Consequently, those who have invested their time toward achieving high grades are the ones the employer will consider first for the company. Therefore, it is reasonable to assume that having a 'want to' attitude will propel you further in life than a 'have to.' Employers are more likely to hire those with a 'want to' work philosophy than those with a 'have to' work philosophy.

Employers understand that people with a 'have to' mindset need to be pushed and constantly motivated by others to accomplish work. In contrast, people with a 'want to' mindset take on responsibilities because they know it is the best way to execute projects. Furthermore, employers invest significant time and resources in educating newly hired employees and want to hire the best from the start. It is called 'getting up to speed with the company,' and the time needed to understand what others already know is called 'the learning curve.'

Knowing these two aspects of every business (getting up to speed and the learning curve), no successful company wants to spend more money, time, and resources to motivate someone they hire. Hired employees should start their new job motivated to be part of the company. 'Want to' employees excel in both aspects; 'have to' employees do not. Consequently, if you view your tasks as something you 'have to' do, you will not likely excel in your academic assignments or work projects, especially those you've been hired for.

Let's consider this from a different perspective. Imagine you own a business and want it to be successful. In that case, you would hire the best person for every position. You would look for someone passionate about their work and who approaches their responsibilities as something they 'want to' do rather than something they 'have to' do. As the hiring manager, you would be interested in knowing how seriously they took their academic education and prior work projects, and what they gained from each. A way of doing this would be to look at their grades and work reviews.

As the hiring manager for your company, you will want to know these things because they will give you a better picture of the kind of person you're hiring. Considering this, the real question is, as of today, would you hire yourself, or would you look for someone more committed to their education and what they are responsible for? This is a moment for self-reflection. If you do not hire yourself, it's time to change your attitude toward learning and working. Start taking your education more seriously and view it as a 'want to' and not a 'have to.'

I want to share an observation about individuals who take education and their future careers seriously. These individuals are guided by ethics and integrity, choosing to do what is right rather than following others' actions. They adhere to rules and guidelines because they believe in fairness for everyone. This type of person has a proactive thought process and understands the importance of boundaries and limitations. They are the 'want to' individuals. They recognize that a person's responsibilities should not change simply because others disregard them.

On the other hand, people who regularly do not follow regulated rules and guidelines but instead use their personal views on what suits their needs in specific places and, at certain times, create inconsistencies, conflicts, or safety concerns, as their actions might not align with established standards designed to ensure fairness, order, and security for everyone. These people do not care for boundaries and feel they are not obligated to adhere to rules because others are breaking them and getting away with it. They are the 'have to' individuals. This being said, remember that ethical behavior is not a choice; it's a significant component of a 'want to' attitude and is crucial for career success. Consequently, your actions carry weight and can either propel you forward or hold you back.

The following exemplifies how progression starts by building poor habits and differentiates between 'have to' and 'want to' perspectives. Suppose students are gathered by the classroom door a few minutes before the bell rings. A person near the door opens the door and slides out about 30 seconds early. The second person witnesses the first person leave and turns to see if the teacher has noticed; if not, the second person slips out before the bell rings.

If you are the second person, do not follow the first who sets a poor example. Furthermore, if the second person (you) desires to be successful and would not have left without an example from the first, continue to be that same person. Do the right thing at the right time. Moreover, remember that your best chances to excel in higher education, gain a stable career, finance a lovely home, and support a beautiful family will not come from following the 'have to' individuals, as they project very little self-motivation and self-discipline.

When the second person gets away with unacceptable behavior, the more they set themselves up to resemble a 'have to' perspective. They increase their chances of becoming the first person who does not care about rules and, as a result, leads others to fault them. Over time, bad habits become the norm for that second person and spread to other areas of their life, such as leaving work early because others do. And no boss wants to micromanage an employee who clock-watches or thinks it's okay to leave the first sign someone else does. These long-term consequences should serve as a deterrent to following poor examples.

The view of life in this age is that getting away with things is standard. Many lie, cheat, steal, or manipulate to better their cause. This occurs because it's not feasible to continuously monitor everyone throughout the day. Therefore, getting away with things like littering, speeding, leaving work early, and vandalism often happens. This is why you need to personally enforce your limits and boundaries to adhere to an ethical atmosphere. If you are at school, some rules apply. If you are at work, some rules apply. If you are driving a vehicle on the road, some restrictions apply.

Leaving class early, before the bell rings, may not seem like a big deal, especially if others are doing it too. However, if you take a moment to reflect on it and the thought process that led to it, you will realize that this is an impulsive decision that will lead to poorer judgments. Over time, if you routinely leave class early, this behavior will become habitual. To avoid this, it's important to exercise self-discipline and resist the temptation to leave early, as this can lead to a sense of arrogance and the belief that it's acceptable to walk out before the bell simply because you've done it before.

From every perspective, your actions will tell you it's okay to violate other things more frequently because your arrogance leads you to believe you can. You will begin forming false, deceptive, and defiant thinking patterns because you will see that your actions have become skewed in your favor. This will only lead to taking more opportunities in your favor, putting you on a fast track to nowhere. I advise you to refrain from this behavior, which can only lead to adverse long-term consequences. One of them is gradually embracing a 'have to' philosophy, where you feel drudgery in working toward accomplishments. This 'have to' attitude often supports poor decisions.

The cost of repairing mistakes caused by poor habits can be high. While they may seem inexpensive initially, the consequences will eventually catch up with you. Poor decisions can lead to even greater damage over time. That's why it's crucial to excel in your responsibilities, whether they are academic, social, or professional. By doing so, you are investing in a more promising future. Focus on performing your duties well. If you find yourself with no responsibilities, seek out some. Aim to be someone who 'wants to' be challenged.

Make it a priority to absorb as much knowledge and understanding as possible before transitioning from your education to a career. Remember that employers will pay you based on the knowledge you have acquired. Meaning, the more you learn, the more you can earn. Your growth and success are directly tied to your knowledge and understanding of that knowledge. If you do not invest in learning, employers will recognize this and compensate you accordingly. The potential for disappointment with future employment due to poor past efforts will be accurate. Be a 'want to' person who motivates others, not a 'have to' person who needs to be motivated.

Critical Thinking and Respect

Respect, a complex concept, is more than just acknowledging the lives and choices of others. It's a personal virtue and a crucial aspect of human interaction with significant societal value. Respect, however, is not a one-dimensional concept. It's about understanding and appreciating others on a deeper level. For some, respect is about having positive feelings or esteem for others, but for others, it holds a deeper significance. Critical thinking is key to understanding this multifaceted nature of respect.

Respect involves recognizing the complete individual and understanding their life circumstances. Thus, valuing the lives of others includes appreciating their efforts, thoughts, and the time they dedicate. This is what we mean by respecting someone. Additionally, respect involves showing compassion, concern, and consideration for another person's needs and feelings. Therefore, showing respect is about following high standards of acceptable societal norms while employing critical thinking.

Critical thinking is not just a theoretical concept; it plays a vital role in helping us understand and empathize with others' needs and feelings. It encourages us to consider different perspectives, which in turn cultivates meaningful interactions and strengthens our relationships. Unlike innate qualities, critical thinking skills are learned and developed through practice. Therefore, growing these skills requires a mindful approach that centers on the well-being and concerns of those around us.

Our understanding of respect is frequently shaped by the examples of influential figures in our lives, such as parents, caregivers, mentors, and even public figures. This form of learning, known as observational learning, is one of the most prevalent ways to acquire this critical value. By closely observing how these role models engage with others—demonstrating kindness, active listening, and empathy—we internalize the principles of respect.

As we mature, our capacity to extend respect not only to others but also to ourselves becomes a skill that can be nurtured and refined over time. This process mirrors the development of critical thinking skills; both require ongoing practice and reflection. We can enhance our interpersonal relationships and foster a more harmonious environment by consciously choosing to emulate respectful behaviors and attitudes. This evolution in our understanding of respect is vital for personal growth and cultivating healthy, meaningful connections.

The more attention we give to understanding the meaning of 'respect' and to sharing its purpose, the more those learning from us will comprehend its significance and value in society. By integrating reflection and critical thinking into our understanding of 'respect,' we can better equip those who learn from us as they begin to navigate life's challenges and face new situations that require respect. As young adults, the traditional, simplistic concept of respect has already set its boundaries and limitations, and because of this, there is a likelihood of deviance from their understanding of complete respect and its deeper meaning.

Demonstrating respect is often associated with specific behaviors and phrases, such as saying 'thank you,' offering a smile of affirmation, maintaining direct (or indirect) eye contact, and executing a firm handshake. These gestures often serve as universal indicators of respect across many cultures. However, it's essential to apply critical thinking to assess the many ways respect is expressed across different cultural contexts, as norms and interpretations of respect can vary significantly.

Understanding respect in different cultural contexts is crucial. For instance, in certain cultures, remaining quiet or maintaining silence in conversation can be interpreted as a profound sign of respect, particularly in the presence of authority figures or during solemn occasions. In some cultures, a lively discussion in which both people playfully interrupt and talk over each other can signify respect, as it shows that both individuals are fully engaged. This cultural distinction underscores the importance of understanding the diverse landscapes of social etiquette.

Moreover, body language and personal space can influence how respect is conveyed and perceived. Therefore, it is pivotal to be mindful of our actions and their potential impact on others. By embracing this understanding, we expand our awareness of what it means to show respect and foster empathy in our interactions, allowing for more meaningful and harmonious relationships across cultural divides.

Understanding the breadth of 'respect' requires critical thinking, as this concept can be complex and often overlooked at first glance. For instance, when one person asks another to meet for an appointment and the second person fails to arrive, the one who did not show up is seen as inconsiderate. However, a deeper examination of this situation reveals an underlying issue of broken mutual respect that both parties overlook. Thus, critical thinking empowers us to navigate such situations and understand the nuances of respect.

In the first place, waiting for someone who fails to show up can lead to a loss of respect. The waiting individual may begin to see the other in a less favorable light, leading to diminished tolerance for the other's future actions. In the second place, the person who missed the appointment undermines their self-respect by not following through. This not only creates a small rift between the two but also poses a challenge that must be addressed if their relationship is to move forward.

A person with critical thinking skills will understand how others feel when their time is wasted and avoid the negative outcome by keeping appointments and being on time. People who show respect to others in this manner do so because they recognize that each person's time is valuable. Similarly, in group discussions, a person with well-developed critical thinking skills will respect others' opinions even if they disagree. People who show respect to others do so because they recognize that each person's perspective is valuable.

In simple terms, critical thinking can be seen as 'good' thinking. It is closely tied to the values of thoughtfulness and encompasses concepts of caring and respect. Enhancing critical thinking can lead to personal growth and a greater capacity to foster more serious respect for others. Together, these qualities lay a strong foundation for making better decisions in all areas of life.

Developing respect for others will lead to a more serious respect within those who display it. Accordingly, the areas where people surround themselves with respect, such as their workplaces, friendships, and communities, will become healthier as they project respectfulness. Consequently, everyone’s commitment to respect and critical thinking is vital in maintaining healthy relationships and contributing to the health of the larger community.

In summary, developing strong critical thinking skills provides a solid foundation for understanding respect. It allows one to value and appreciate another's views and ideas, even in disagreement. Therefore, critical thinking will enable you to examine opinions without bias, allowing for a deeper understanding of differing perspectives. When we show respect for others, we do not judge them based on their attitudes, thoughts, or behaviors. Instead, we accept them as they are without expecting them to change.

What is your definition of *discipline*? Write clearly and concisely here:

How is *discipline* tied to critical thinking?

How has your *discipline* (or lack of) impacted your life up to this point?

How do critical thinking skills strengthen a person's sense of *discipline?*

Explain how developing a progressive sense of *discipline* can positively impact a person's life.

Explain how the absence of developing a sense of *discipline* may hurt a person's life. (For instance, avoiding potential dangers, understanding personal emotions, etc.)

Express how you feel about *discipline* being one of the most essential things in a successful life. (You may need to define the term successful)

Chapter 9
Time and Traffic Lights Are Equalizers

Have patience with all things but first of all with yourself.

— **Francis de Sales.**

Two things define you: your patience when you have nothing and your attitude when you have everything.

— **George Bernard Shaw**

Taking your time during important life events is significant. When we allow ourselves the necessary time to do things properly, we gain invaluable lessons that shape our future. Consequently, life's important moments should be filled with meaning and purpose; otherwise, the time we invest can feel wasted. No one intentionally wants to waste their time, but when events are rushed and lack a clear purpose, they become mere moments rather than meaningful experiences.

When you tackle critical events with the purposeful intention and dedication they deserve, events will transform into valuable experiences. Furthermore, reflecting on these experiences deepens your understanding and brings a sense of fulfillment, inspiring and motivating you to achieve more. Consequently, a large part of accomplishing anything in life lies in the knowledge and insights gained from reflecting on your experiences. This is why events done with purpose are so important.

Taking the time to reflect on our experiences is essential. When we rush through without pausing to think, we risk overlooking the deeper significance of our involvement. For instance, if you hurry through a job interview or a skill-building project designed to teach valuable career lessons, you may not fully understand the essential elements that could benefit you in future experiences. Therefore, it's important to invest time in working toward goals and enjoying the rewards they bring. If others rush through their tasks without recognizing the benefits, that's their choice. Hence, the heading of this chapter, Time and Traffic Lights, serves as a great equalizer.

Suppose you complete a bachelor's degree in one year. You would need to complete courses four times as fast as if you took the standard route to a bachelor's degree in four years. Taking the one-year route would be less impactful than remaining on a structured four-year timeline. Taking the courses on a reasonable four-year plan will give you time to discuss topics, reflect on the material, and create meaningful research. Separating the coursework over four years will allow for gradual knowledge acquisition, provide time to gather materials, and allow thorough preparation for and reflection on quizzes and tests at timely intervals.

The standard four years provides time to process the relevance of assignments, debate concepts in needed discussions, and reflect on the material presented in the courses. It also offers ample time to gain perspective on work and apply what is learned in the real world before graduation. Furthermore, the standard four-year route to a bachelor's degree allows you to gain some depth in understanding how your chosen field fits into your life. Rushing through a bachelor's degree in one year does not allow for reflection on the material. Thus, you will have only short-term information, which will be difficult, if not impossible, to apply.

This comparison of rushing through an academic degree and gaining very little substance can be related to living life in general. Remember, you don't need to rush through life as many others seem to. If you do, you'll find that time will eventually create an equalizing experience. Those who rushed ahead will inevitably be stalled for one reason or another, while those who took their time will catch up. Whether people hurry or take their time, they will cross paths again.

Those who hurry often fail to grasp their goals fully, so when they dive into life's events too soon, they end up taking longer to get from point A to point B. On the other hand, those who approach situations methodically—spending time to understand the circumstances before acting—may start their journey a bit later. Still, ultimately, they find a quicker path from point A to point B. Ultimately, both groups typically arrive at point B around the same time.

This concept can be further illustrated with an example of assembling an item with instructions. It is often the case that those who rush through the instructions end up taking much longer to put an item together. In contrast, the methodical take their time reading all the necessary information and quickly and efficiently assemble the item. Therefore, my advice for you regarding life is to gather knowledge and develop understanding before you leap into adventures. It is wise to take this route because life is about reaching destinations and appreciating the processes and the lessons they bring.

In keeping with the theme of education and the idea that time is a great equalizer, those who rush through their education only to acquire knowledge may lose sight of the importance of genuinely engaging with the material presented. As a result, those who rush may spend a couple of years bouncing from job to job, trying to find the right fit because they do not understand their knowledge base and how it can be applied to a meaningful career.

On the other hand, those who take the time to earn a meaningful four-year degree will have a richer perspective on the material covered and, thus, a better handle on where their knowledge base fits best in the field they enter. Therefore, time is a great equalizer, balancing out those who rush their understanding and bounce from job to job before landing a career and those who are methodical in developing a sense of their knowledge and finding a well-suited career early. Therefore, in hindsight, take your time and do things right. The power to shape your future is in your hands.

It's crucial to allow moments of pause between life events to reflect on what has happened. Meaningful reflection is a necessary but often overlooked process. It provides perspective on what has happened and helps plan for what's next. Taking time to reflect on your next steps can deepen the value and significance of your past achievements and set you up for productive future steps. It's essential to avoid activities that don't contribute to your personal success, as reflecting on how you've wasted time can lead to even more wasted time.

Keep in mind that reflection can be applied to any aspect of your life, including the friendships you maintain. By examining past friendships and current friendships, you can gain valuable insight into how you should monitor your relationships and interactions. Consider the following questions in your reflection: What have I learned from my friends? What do I do when I am around them? Do they have any goals or ambitions, and if so, do they put any effort behind them?

If you're considering a new friendship, take it slow and apply the wisdom you've gained from past experiences. Rushing into a friendship may prevent a bond from forming. Thus, reflecting on past friendships equips you with knowledge and awareness as you move into a new friendship, making you a wiser and more thoughtful friend. Time, as an equalizer, also applies here: rushed friendships begin quickly and often fade, whereas those that develop slowly tend to be longer-lasting. Those who rush build bonds sooner than those who take their time; however, those who take their time end up with a more rewarding relationship.

Let's look at time as an equalizer with career choices. Consider the following questions: Why are you working at this place? Who influences you at your work? How long do you see yourself working here? What skills are you gaining by working at this place? Before accepting a future job, take a moment to consider whether it's a role where you can excel. Reflecting on these questions can enhance your sense of control and confidence in your career path. Rushing to accept a job offer may provide a place to work much sooner than others who are contemplating their next move. However, taking the time to thoughtfully consider their next move can lead to greater satisfaction with their decision and may result in a more enduring placement.

When you end a relationship or leave a career, take your time before transitioning into the next one. This transition time should not be considered a poor use of time, but a time to learn about yourself and prepare for what awaits you in your next relationship or career. Reflecting on past events provides insight and perspective on how improvements can be made and what should be avoided. Thus, time is a great equalizer between those who rush into and out of events and those who take time to reflect on them. Those who rush in and out of personal relationships and jobs may experience a lot in a short time. However, those who take the time to think things through before stepping into these areas often find their relationships and careers become more fulfilling and meaningful.

Everything you do influences you in some manner—whether physically, mentally, spiritually, emotionally, or socially. This underscores the importance of reflecting on your actions. Taking time to reflect allows you to decompress and analyze thoughts, preventing you from hastily jumping into your next event and possibly squandering your time. Although it may feel like you are lagging behind those who quickly move on to their next event, engaging in reflection will ultimately position you for tremendous success in the long run.

Keep in mind the passage of time rewards those who reflect. Those who pause to think critically about life's events catch up and surpass those who rush through them. This occurs because rushing can trap individuals in a cycle of making poor decisions, leading to complications. To correct this, they need to either slow down or reflect. With that in mind, it's crucial to take a moment to think things through before making decisions, particularly when it comes to significant life changes. It's worth mentioning that not every event in life calls for reflection. However, making a habit of reflecting—even on the small moments—can be beneficial.

For example, it will take only a few moments to reflect after returning home from the grocery store and remembering you forgot to get something important. After reflecting, write the item's name down to remember it next time. In your reflection, you may also realize you can grab a few other items to save another trip. A quick reflection such as this does not need to be drawn out; therefore, pause and then move on with your day, leaving the reflection of that event to rest.

However, more significant events will require more reflection, such as returning quickly home from the grocery store and reflecting on the collision that almost happened between your vehicle and another driver. Maybe you were in a hurry or unaware of your surroundings. At any rate, tires screeched, and horns blared. The stress, anxiety, and recounting of the moments from this event will stay with you for a while since it was dramatic. Your reflection on this event will take some time to dissipate.

With this kind of event, analyzing who had the right of way and what could have been done to prevent the incident is normal. Your mind will ponder this incident periodically in the days and weeks ahead, helping ensure that similar incidents are not taken lightly, and that more attention is paid to avoiding them. However, because of this saturated attention to this event, other events you want to consider about your day will not get equal attention.

Again, we return to the concept of time being the great equalizer. In the first case of returning casually home from the grocery store, you could continue your day with only a short reflection on the items you forgot to get. However, in the second case of returning home quickly from the grocery store, your mind must decompress from the ordeal you experienced, leading to a more extended, more drawn-out reflection.

You end up in the same place in both scenarios above because time is a great equalizer. In the first scenario, you took longer from point A, the store, to point B, home, and a short reflection. The second scenario was shorter from point A, the store, to point B, home, and a more extended reflection regarding the incident. Thus, things in life have a way of equaling out; time is the great equalizer. Therefore, take your time and do things methodically; it will bring a sense of calm and control to your life. Don't worry about others who seem to be rushing ahead of you.

Rushing through events will only put you in a defensive position when the next event begins. This is because you will be forced to stop and reflect longer to resolve deeper issues, or to return to a point to redo what you rushed through. I have fallen into this situation before, needing to return to my past to gather more information and build knowledge before moving forward. Rushing through life's events never works out. This is why time is a great equalizer for those who have rushed through life's events. Time will slow the overzealous down to a crawl, having to repeat things in life.

Take the time you need and put in the effort on your initial attempts to avoid having to return and redo your work. Remember, time waits for no one. If you don't complete projects on time or fail to meet expectations because you're overloaded or distracted by other things, the world won't pause to give you a chance to recover from missed deadlines. Time keeps moving forward, and those who manage their tasks effectively—by avoiding overload and not trying to accomplish everything at once—will finish their projects on time and stay ahead of the game.

Eventually, time will catch up with those who race ahead without reflecting on how they achieved their goals. Consequently, the constant pressure of time allows slower, more methodical people to catch up to those who have rushed through part of their lives. Therefore, take time and do things correctly, efficiently, and methodically. It is the best way to keep advancing and building confidence. You will have the best of both worlds: more knowledge and understanding of your accomplishments, stronger self-confidence, and better reflective thinking skills.

If I can impart some wisdom to you about achieving your goals and working through events systematically, it would be to let them be personal. Allow your goals to resonate with you by taking your time to complete them to the best of your ability. Let the things you are working on be part of your daily schedule, something you have made room for, not something you quickly do on the side only to put them past you. Allow your ambitions and goals to be personal, so you become fully invested in working with them at a high level.

This chapter is all about doing things right the first time. There's no need to go back and repeat what's already been done. Repeating events in your life will only hinder you. Those who take their time and don't skip steps while working towards their goals may seem behind those who rush ahead. However, as time passes, those who continue to rush will be put in a situation where they must redo their work.

In contrast, those who performed the same or similar events methodically and correctly the first time will slowly advance, while those who rushed through them will fall behind. As they narrow the gap, they'll feel more confident in their achievements and be in a stronger position to overtake those who got ahead early. Ask any successful person, and they'll tell you—a unique sense of confidence and pride is a strong catalyst for momentum, and it comes from knowing you've done your best.

Consider this analogy: when building a fence, ensure that each primary post is firmly anchored. Allow the cement to set properly and let each post stand straight and firm before adding the horizontal 2x4s and vertical fence slats. Consequently, if you complete a work project to the best of your ability the first time, you will save time by not having to redo it. You heard the phrase 'haste makes waste.' Well, it's true. Doing things too quickly creates more potential for errors, and as a result, those errors will slow you down. Performing the same work a second time wastes your first efforts.

The passage of time can put things in perspective if you don't do things correctly when you have the chance. Furthermore, if you anticipate advancing in life but have not done things correctly in the past when given the opportunity, time will not stop while you fix them. I have seen and heard many people fall into the trap of being overzealous and opinionated about their quick successes and accomplishments, only to have their achievements fall apart and be worth much less. To salvage their accomplishments, their only option is to return and correct them.

Regarding the above scenario of 'haste makes waste,' it is also important to avoid arrogance when you find yourself ahead of others. Avoid this because life has a way of balancing one individual's events with another's. Life has an uncanny knack for balancing the scales of fortune and misfortune across individuals, regardless of being methodical and doing things correctly. Therefore, it's wise to remember that your current successes may be fleeting and that circumstances can change unexpectedly. Life is full of timing, luck, and chance.

So, what does this have to do with traffic lights? Traffic lights are like checkpoints along the road of life. The lights represent moments in a person's life where they can cruise through on green if they have made thoughtful, reflective, and sensible decisions, feeling empowered and confident. The lights also represent moments in a person's life when they need to wait at a red light to make corrections, fixing hasty decisions that led to mistakes.

In life, those who rush through their decisions and tasks may appear ahead at the start, but they often find themselves stuck at the 'red lights' down the road, needing to correct their mistakes. Meanwhile, those who do things correctly and reflect on their actions are methodically progressing through the 'green lights,' steadily closing the gap and catching up.

Time is an equalizer that balances the fast pace of others and their mistakes with those of slower, more methodical people. It's like a series of traffic lights that regulate traffic flow. Suppose two cars are traveling down the street in the same direction and are headed to the same destination. The destination is a long way out, and getting there will take some time. One vehicle travels at the posted speed limit, while the second vehicle ignores it and moves much faster.

The second vehicle, exceeding the speed limit, quickly accelerates away from the first vehicle after the traffic light turns green, reaching the next traffic light. The second vehicle covers more ground more quickly between traffic lights, but also runs the risk of being pulled over and given a speeding citation. After several intersections with traffic lights, the second vehicle has increased its distance from the first and passes through several more. As luck would have it, the second vehicle caught a couple of green lights in a row.

Then, as the odds would have it, or as life would have it, the second vehicle is pulled over by law enforcement and cited with a traffic violation for speeding. While pulled over, the first vehicle, obeying the speed limit, overtakes the second vehicle, which is still being detained. Not only did the first overtake the second, but the second also encountered more hurdles and delays than the first. The second driver now must address issues arising from the traffic citation.

The second driver may face a high insurance premium, spend time in court trying to reduce the ticket, and/or take a defensive driving course. These added burdens can significantly affect their life. Meanwhile, the first driver, who is following the rules (doing things correctly), is far ahead. I have witnessed this scenario multiple times with friends and realized there is no advantage in speeding on the road or 'through life' when the outcomes could ultimately slow down one's future.

Life's randomness often balances gains with losses and fairness with cheating, much as traffic lights bring racers back to an equal position alongside those they pass. Elusiveness and deception operate in much the same way. No shortcuts allow someone to advance and keep moving ahead without facing some form of compensation, retribution, or equality. Taking shortcuts rarely, if ever, benefits someone in the long run.

Shortcuts may appear advantageous when people around you acquire more than their share by working the system, bending the rules in their favor, or doing things when others are not looking. But life has a way of equalizing everything. The best advice I can give you is, "Don't follow their lead." Uphold your integrity, take your time, and do things correctly to the best of your ability. Do not worry about how far others appear ahead of you or how much fun they seem to have while cheating the system.

One day, everything will balance out for everyone. Therefore, don't be discouraged by those who are getting ahead by illegal means or taking shortcuts. You need to focus on your work and how you want it to turn out. Some people may undervalue their future and be unaware of the sacrifices they make by taking shortcuts. But don't let this mindset be yours. This chapter aims to help you become more conscious of your choices and how making the right ones can build a more solid, stable foundation. Therefore, having to go back and correct mistakes or compensate for hasty decisions will hinder your progress more than staying on course and doing things correctly from the start.

Let's talk about a few specific aspects of life and the concept of time. Suppose you turn in a course assignment or a final project for work, which is returned with a poor grade or is labeled an incomplete project. In this case, you may have put yourself in a position to work much harder on the next assignment to make up the missed points. Regarding the work project, you may have put yourself in a position among those employees that others view as taking shortcuts. And it might take some time and a few more work projects to cancel people's initial view of your previous turn-in.

The best advice is to avoid shortcuts and quick turn-ins. If a shortcut has worked for you once, you might be tempted to use it again. Thus, over time, relying on shortcuts can become habitual, leading you to believe they save you time. However, there is a greater chance that shortcuts will fail, which could cost you more time and effort to fix than if you had not taken a shortcut. This simple illustration shows that avoiding shortcuts is wise, especially when making more significant life decisions.

If you like numbers, this illustration is for you. When rushing through life's events, you may win some and lose some, depending on what you take away from your experiences and can apply to the future. Remember, you will have better success taking your time with events you encounter and reflecting on their significance as you transition into new life events than moving too quickly onto the next event without reflection. Winning once and failing once (going back to make corrections) is a 50% success rate, which is extremely low. Why not perform events correctly and without shortcuts so the first and second average a 100% success rate? You may arrive at the 100% success rate a little later than others in life and after some reflection, but when all is said and done, you have 100% to be proud of.

The concept of time being a great equalizer can also be seen in professional careers and sports. For example, a person climbs the corporate ladder a couple of rungs because their motivation is money and status, only to find they have yet to understand what makes the company work. This person will realize they cannot advance their career further, as they have not gained corporate experience.

In sports where athletes use illegal substances to gain an advantage over their competition, they eventually find out they are in jeopardy of being suspended or released from their team. This could result in loss of contract, fame, and endorsements. In contrast to these two professions, those who have climbed the ladder to success by gaining an understanding of their company and those athletes who have worked hard to become better without substance are the ones who will move much further past the others who are taking shortcuts.

The concept of time being a great equalizer can also be seen in relationships. Rushing into relationships can lead to adverse outcomes, highlighting the importance of taking time to develop connections. Relationships based on superficial attraction often fade more quickly than those built on shared interests that develop as you get to know each other. As a result, stable relationships grounded in shared interests usually grow stronger and lead to more lasting commitments.

Marrying the right person is paramount to nearly everyone who wants a happy life with a loving spouse and the possibility of building a family. Quickly marrying a person for superficial criteria often hurts both parties. A quick engagement and marriage may come at the cost of a divorce shortly after. Those who hastily enter marriage and quickly start a family without a foundation of mutual understanding, common goals, ambitions, or a deep commitment to each other will often find it challenging to sustain the marriage. However, taking the time to truly understand the person you plan to marry and what both of you want and need from the marriage can pave the way for a longer and more fulfilling partnership.

Couples who take the time to nurture a relationship and work through their differences and personal issues often grow to love each other deeply. As a result, they may start their families later than couples who rush into marriage. However, the couple that has taken their time in this process is often better positioned for a longer, happier marriage. Of course, deciding to rush into marriage versus taking time involves many other variables and factors. Nonetheless, those who take their time generally have a better chance of enjoying a long-lasting and fulfilling marriage.

The concept of time being a great equalizer can also be seen in finance. The quick and easy payoff often results in setbacks. This is the rushed approach to building wealth. However, a systematic and methodical approach to investing, focusing on small gains over time, can provide a profound sense of control and stability. This is not to say that small gains are correct and quick opportunities are wrong. But, in the long run, slow gains will overcome the ups and downs of possible quick profits. This is because a fast buck by taking shortcuts or betting on 'sure investments' rarely works.

Those in the financial game who want to score big rarely put limits on their gains; instead, they aim for bigger, more significant gains. To them, there is never enough, and it cannot come fast enough. When they fail, they find themselves in a worse financial and emotional position than if they had taken a slower, systematic, and methodical approach. While the slow-and-steady approach may not provide instant gratification, it can lead to a profound sense of control and empowerment over one's financial future. Thus, the passage of time can bridge the gap between the quick, sporadic gains of living life and the steady, slow-paced achievements.

In summary, time is all you have in this world, so optimize it. Make it work for you by being careful about what you do and how consistently you do it. Do not worry about others who seem to be racing ahead of you, acquiring things you wish you had or are working for. Instead, focus on making your moves count so you will not need to return at any point in your life and repeat processes you have already performed. The goal is to avoid the need to repeat work.

Metaphorically speaking, you do not want to be stopped at 'traffic lights' because of a mistake caused by your hasty decisions. By making your moves carefully, methodically, and correctly the first time, you will eventually have what others have with fewer second efforts. And if you still want what others have, you will have plenty of opportunities to acquire it due to your more stable position.

If you are in school or taking courses independently, do your best to graduate and put it behind you. Do your best to avoid dropping out and needing to repeat your academic efforts later. Get the initial diploma now by doing your work right the first time. If you are in college, commit to passing each course you register for. Do your best to avoid distractions that will jeopardize your efforts.

Furthermore, when embarking on a new job or career, it's crucial to demonstrate your commitment to the organization's success right from the start. Make a concerted effort to contribute positively to the workplace culture and objectives, showcasing your initiative and dedication.

It's equally important to practice professional etiquette that fosters a respectful environment. For instance, strive to arrive on time consistently, as punctuality reflects your reliability and respect for your colleagues and the company's time. Additionally, refrain from engaging in negative conversations about coworkers or the organization. Such behavior can create a toxic atmosphere and harm your reputation.

As mentioned earlier, taking your time and doing things correctly to the best of your ability will not guarantee that everything you do will be perfect; you will still need to return to some things and rework or resolve them, such as an assignment, work project, poorly ended friendship, and others. Going back to redo or resolve things helps us remember that while recovery from an initial misstep or hasty decision remains possible, it often requires humility, patience, and a willingness to grow. These moments remind us that progress is not measured by flawless performance but by our capacity to acknowledge mistakes, make adjustments, and continue moving forward with greater clarity.

Recognizing the value of revisiting our mistakes doesn't mean every situation can be easily repaired. In some cases, such as creating a poor first impression, the opportunity to correct course is far more limited. Attempting to reshape a poor first impression often comes across as insincere or manipulative. First impressions carry significant weight and set the tone for future interactions. Therefore, prioritize exhibiting integrity and a genuine desire to contribute positively to the workplace from day one.

I realized that much of this section was on work, school, and driving, but this concept applies to every area of life. I leave the contemplation regarding how and where to use this concept up to you. The basic idea is not worrying about others and their progress toward their goals, their standing in life, or whether they seem much further ahead than you are.

Moreover, don't think too highly of yourself for being ahead of others. There are many ups and downs, and twists and turns, that separate everyone's ability to perform and why they perform. Everyone has their unique ways of relating to and navigating through life. Life can change a person's circumstances instantly, and someone behind you now may surpass you later. Consequently, it is also true that arrogant people can be hindered by their egos, allowing those with a different perspective on life to pass them by.

Chapter 10
Ten Thousand Hours

If you do the work, you get rewarded. There are no shortcuts in life.

— **Michael Jordan**

Let me share the ten-thousand-hour rule if you have not heard it. It is a non-scientific, generally accepted rule that represents the time required to master a talent and achieve a high level of competence. The concept holds that putting in 10,000 hours of progressive practice will achieve mastery at the highest level. The rule is not restricted to any specific area of life but can serve as a guide, showing that with time, effort, and perseverance, you can accomplish anything exceptionally well.

This rule of reaching personal success has been applied to athletes, professional careers, rock musicians, and their claims to fame. The ten-thousand-hour rule can also apply in academia, where doctoral degree holders have spent much of their time researching and becoming experts in their fields. However, the rule has some limitations: the time spent must be consistent, and the work must be progressive.

The concept of 'ten thousand hours' emphasizes that it takes persistence and dedication to achieve anything worthwhile. Goals that require significant time and effort are usually the most rewarding. Demonstrating high performance in any field—sports, music, or education—

reflects your commitment and passion. Everyone has the potential to excel in whatever they choose to pursue. I encourage you to discover and strive to become the best at something you enjoy.

However, being the best is more than this; it's about passion. You must stay on track with your goals and invest time and effort to be the best. Having the continued passion to persist is a large part of success. Understandably, other things will capture your interest over time. During these moments, you must continue to put time and energy into what you have already started. It's not always easy to refrain from taking tangents. These will be your most challenging obstacles in reaching success.

When you focus on your main passion, adding other interests can distract you. Picking up new goals may sidetrack your first passion. If you are sidetracked for a while and lose interest altogether, you will most likely give up on your passion. Depending on how much time has passed, if you regain interest, you may need to start your 10,000-hour count over from the beginning. This being noted, the ambitious and motivated go-getters who continue the path they started and do not allow distractions from other interests to derail them are the ones who become the best at what they do.

It would help if you said 'no' to many things as you work to achieve greatness in your first passion. Saying 'no' means consistently choosing your specific passion over various distractions. For example, if you say 'no' to spending 4 hours a day on your phone, you allow more time for your passion.

By saying 'no' to hanging out with friends all the time, you create space in your schedule to focus on your ambitions.

If you want to be excellent at playing the guitar or drums or become a talented writer or artist, you are effectively saying 'yes' to your goals each time you say 'no' to less important activities. This process involves prioritizing what you feel is important based on its value and significance. By continually choosing the first passion or ambition you have been focusing on repeatedly, you become much better at saying no to less ambitious things.

By adding up the hours you have dedicated to your ambition, you'll notice they accumulate quickly. By saying 'no' to insignificant distractions and 'yes' to spending more time pursuing your goals, you distance yourself from those who invest only occasional time in self-improvement. The extra hours you dedicate to mastering a skill will far surpass the hours others have contributed to the same pursuit.

Eventually, you become much better at what you do than others, and you put yourself in the ranks of professionals of your chosen talent. To truly be great means dedicating your time and energy to a single pursuit, letting go of all other distractions, and consistently honing your focus on that one thing continually. When reaching for this top rung, you need to ask yourself two questions, and the answer to them must be the same each day you ask them: How bad do you want it? And what are you willing to sacrifice to get it?

For this chapter, I have limited my examples to sports and music because they lend themselves more readily to the ten-thousand-hour rule. However, the concept can be applied to anything you work toward, such as learning a foreign language, mastering a craft like woodworking, or becoming a gifted artist. Additionally, the ten thousand hours is a ballpark number. It isn't like someone will hand you a certificate of mastery for your chosen talent after you complete 10,000 hours of practice.

Receiving a certificate for ten thousand hours will never happen. What will happen is experiencing the personal growth and self-discovery that come with the journey of mastery. Nobody will give you a certificate of completion. This is because your effort and work are personal and take many forms. Hence, you might be the only one keeping track of the time spent learning and mastering your talent. However, you will also be the one who experiences the most profound changes and insights.

The changes in your growth and the insight you have gained along the way will be priceless. You will only know the incremental progress made daily, weekly, and month after month. In the words of Michael Chandler, a professional mixed martial artist, patience and determination are enough to see your goal through to the end. This phrase emphasizes the importance of perseverance and consistency in skill development, which are critical and foundational principles of the ten-thousand-hour rule.

Ten thousand hours of practice is a logical and sensible way to interpret your sustained effort toward a specific goal. But it is not a universal truth for everyone who takes a journey to become proficient in a talent or craft they choose.

Only some who work toward the limit will be rewarded equally with time relative to progress. Some may be rewarded with rapid progression as their proficiency grows faster than expected. However, some may be rewarded at much slower increments as their proficiency develops. Ultimately, each person's growth trajectory is unique.

Each person's learning curve and aptitude for learning are slightly different; therefore, their progress in mastering their passion or ambition will be seen at various times. Some may have an affinity for a specific talent, such as singing, and take to it quickly, while others will need to practice longer and more rigorously to accomplish the same milestones.

One way to think about staggered learning abilities is to imagine two people learning a musical instrument. Some individuals may quickly grasp the basics of an instrument, but then experience a slowdown in their progress over the months. In contrast, others might take longer to understand the foundational elements and mechanics initially, but once they get the hang of it, they often soar in their knowledge and skill.

Everyone learns at different paces, in various ways, and with different motivational styles. This variability is not a sign of failure in anyone but a natural part of the learning process. Consequently, the ten-thousand-hour rule is an estimate. It is a guideline that allows ample time for practice, reflection, processing, and repetition.

A person may be very good at what they do after 10,000 hours, but that is no guarantee they will perform professionally after years of practice. To enhance practice efficiency and increase the chance of reaching a professional level, practice must be purposeful and intentional. Purposeful and intentional practice means focusing on specific aspects of a skill that need improvement, setting clear goals for each practice session, and seeking feedback to identify areas for growth.

The time invested in a craft, whether mastering academics, playing an instrument, singing, or playing a sport, must be consistent and progressive. Consistent means practicing on a regular schedule with regular intervals. Progressive means increasing the time spent practicing and learning new concepts as talent improves. The element of progressiveness makes learning a talent difficult and forms the backbone of a person's skill.

Progressive learning can be thought of like this. Suppose you are learning to play the guitar. You start by learning two or three chords. After some time, you are much better at strumming those two or three chords, but you have not increased the number of chords you are learning. You have been repeating the same two or three chords for months. This is not progressive learning.

Progressive learning would involve learning new chords, mastering them, and then moving on to more complex chords. There are eight different chord types (minor, major, diminished, etc.) in musical instruments, and 12 chords (C, C#, D, D#, E, etc.) represent each note on the musical scale within each type. Mastery involves learning all of them and progressing through their difficult stages.

The idea of consistent learning is evaluated by how effectively you integrate your skills into your daily life. Setting aside time each day is the most effective way to see improvement. I've heard that as little as 20 minutes a day can lead to noticeable progress, but that's likely the minimum time you should dedicate each day. This is important because reaching the ten-thousand-hour milestone will take a significant amount of time at that pace.

Twenty minutes a day, every day, add up to only 122 hours a year. Performing a quick calculation, 10,000 hours divided by 122 hours a year equals a little more than 81 years. Therefore, if you want to improve and be the best at what you do, and do not want it to take 81 years, you will need to invest more time each day than 20 minutes.

Your invested time should be consistent in length and duration for the best results. The length of practice that seems doable for most people is thirty minutes to two hours a day. This window will capitalize on good habits from your previous efforts, incorporate new material, and build muscle memory. For instance, you could spend the first 15 minutes warming up, the next 30 minutes learning new material, and the remaining time practicing what you've learned. Thirty minutes to two hours allows you to learn new skills and practice old ones.

It's crucial to continually push yourself to learn new skills while working toward your craft (passion, ambition, talent) and reviewing previously learned skills. This commitment to growth and learning will keep you motivated and inspired, ensuring you continue to progress. Once again, time spent in practice and the effort to increase your abilities are essential to become proficient. In the words of Leonardo da Vinci, those who accomplish things rarely sit back and observe things happening around them. They are the ones making things happen.

The time you spend between practices is also critical. During this time, your brain muscles remember and process what happened during practice. Our brain muscles combine the information in each learning session and fill the gap between old and new knowledge. This means connecting what you've learned in the past with what you're learning now. The downtime between practices is also valuable to your mind and body recovery. The mind and body must have sufficient time to absorb and recover.

It is impossible to practice for ten thousand hours straight and assume you will master a craft. Your physical muscles and mental awareness must have downtime to grow stronger, adapt to, and process what you are trying to accomplish; thus, it takes time. Therefore, practicing without resting hinders you from learning what you practiced. Furthermore, moving too quickly can, in some cases, lead to less progress. Consequently, success doesn't happen straight out of the gate or overnight.

Success takes time to develop, unlike wealth, which can happen overnight by winning the lottery. However, success is not winning the lottery. Winning the lottery and becoming wealthy overnight takes no more effort than buying a lottery ticket. However, success is built on hard work and discipline, the result of devoted time, effort, and sacrifice. Acquiring ten hours will not be easy.

Stepping up the hours per day will surely shorten the duration to reach ten thousand hours, but at the same time, you run the risk of the brain and muscles not having time to process what has been learned in prior practices. Suppose you practice for 16 hours a day. You made it your sole ambition to do only a few things: eat, sleep, and practice your craft (sports, musical instruments, learning a language, artistry, whatever). By practicing 16 hours, you will reach a ten-thousand-hour goal in just under a year and nine months. But it hardly seems possible to be a professional in any one talent in under two years.

When interviewing athletes and musicians, they say they started practicing as children or young adults and took many years to become proficient. For example, Michael Jordan began practicing basketball at a young age, and it took a decade to reach his greatness. As basketball practice became tiring and he wanted to stop, he would close his eyes momentarily and picture the locker room without his name on any locker. This pushed him to continue his workouts. The thought of being replaced by another talented person made him the best at what he does.

Quickly acquiring the hours is not the way to go. Racing through to master a talent, you will miss out on practicing with others at different stages of ability, where you gain valuable insight into your craft. For instance, a novice musician can learn from an experienced one about the nuances of playing complex melodies. When you race to master a skill, your body cannot adapt quickly enough to build the muscle memory needed to sustain your efforts. Professional piano players, guitar players, saxophone players, etc., have the flexibility in their fingers and the strength in their hands from years of practice playing the most complex combinations of notes. It is impossible to assume a person can crunch all their practices together hour after hour without allowing time between them for mental processing and building dexterity and strength; it takes time.

Mastery needs to be a gradual process that allows your muscles to adapt to specific movements and your brain to process your understanding. The brain reflects on new knowledge and awareness, such as your physical muscles and intellectual abilities, which you gain from the actions and techniques you consistently practice. Ideally, this process unfolds gradually, as it should in a perfect world. However, you may not notice improvement each day or every week. Only over time will you see significant progress.

When practicing day after day, it may seem like individualized practice, with no noticeable improvement. Do not be discouraged with the day-to-day results. This is how things work: noticeable gains are not that obvious day to day, but instead over the long term. Behind the scenes, the brain gathers information about what you are doing and sympathizes with it, creating a smooth learning curve when viewed on a longer timeline. Therefore, you may not notice considerable jumps in learning on certain days, but they will be noticeable when looking back at your first steps.

There will be practice sessions where you might feel that no progress has been made and you've gained no real benefit. This is normal. It happens, and it might happen often. But don't let it discourage you. Trust in the process. Your time spent practicing and your continual effort will pay off. I cannot stress this concept enough. No matter how small or inconsequential the progress might seem, continue working at it, knowing that every practice, no matter how small the gain appears, is a crucial part of the bigger picture in reaching professional status. Your determination and commitment, more than anything else, will lead you to success.

Do you desire to be great at something in your life right now? You may have been inspired by watching others perform at a high level. You may have been motivated by athletes to become an athlete yourself or by musicians to become a musician. If there's a dream of being the best at something on your mind right now, don't wait any longer. Start today to improve on that talent.

Start with just 20 minutes a day, and if you enjoy what you do, keep increasing the time you spend each day. The time to start is now. Let this chapter inspire you to begin your journey toward greatness. The journey starts with a single step, and that step is now. I wrote a saying earlier in this series of books about taking advantage of opportunities, and it also applies here: the best time to have planted a tree was 20 years ago; the second-best time is now. Heading this warning, if you have not built up your talent in the past, it's okay; start now.

Start practicing now while you're young and have plenty of time. Tomorrow will bring more responsibilities, and other obligations will occupy your time. Therefore, carve out time each day now to work toward your dream. If you don't have a specific goal at the moment, focus on being the best you can be in your current activities. Whether in sports, playing an instrument in a band, excelling in your foreign language class, or any other interest, strive to improve and give your best effort. There's no time like the present. Don't wait for the perfect moment; create it now.

Critical Thinking and Creativity

Creativity is an extraordinary process that generates something new from existing ideas or materials. It can be tangible or intangible. The fundamental concept is that something novel emerges from something else. Like innovation, creativity involves generating novel interpretations of original concepts, building upon existing knowledge, and solving challenges. In essence, creativity is the spark that ignites new ideas and inspires us to think innovatively.

Fostering creative thought develops advanced cognitive functions that go beyond foundational thinking skills such as mere recall, comprehension, or the application of information. Creativity flourishes best when paired with critical thinking, especially when it involves careful analysis and comprehensive evaluation. This involves examining ideas and concepts to understand their components and assess their relevance, significance, and potential impact. Individuals can better synthesize new insights and perspectives by cultivating these critical thinking skills, ultimately enhancing their creative capabilities.

Critical thinkers and creative individuals are closely linked through their open-mindedness and willingness to embrace new ideas. They actively seek out novelties and thrive on exploring and testing boundaries. They have an affinity for and appreciate perspectives that differ from traditional views. Their common mindset brings them together, fostering a strong sense of community and belonging within the broader intellectual landscape. Pursuing new ideas and exploring unconventional perspectives are accepted and celebrated here, making them feel valued and appreciated.

The beauty of creative imagination and critical thinking lies in their accessibility to everyone. These skills can be nurtured at any age, challenging the notion that creativity is an innate talent reserved for a select few. Instead, creativity is a skill honed through practice and the application of knowledge. Similarly, well-developed critical thinking results from consistent practice and a deep understanding of various concepts. This journey of developing skills reminds us of the incredible potential within each of us, enabling us to cultivate these skills and enhance our personal growth.

The beauty of creative and critical thinking resides in their capacity to transcend conventional approaches. They empower individuals to delve into uncharted territories of thought and explore innovative concepts and diverse perspectives. Thus, the beauty of creative and critical thinking lies in their ability to move away from routine processes, encouraging individuals to explore new ideas and perspectives.

Creative thinking encourages the generation of original ideas, while critical thinking thoroughly examines them through logical analysis and reflection. Engaging in this ongoing reflective process is crucial for assessing one's beliefs and assumptions about various issues. It enables individuals to distinguish right from wrong while understanding the nuanced implications of these judgments, including their values and the broader societal context. By engaging in this dynamic interplay between creativity and critical analysis, individuals cultivate a deeper understanding of themselves and the complex world around them.

While creativity and critical thinking play significant roles in personal development, they exhibit distinct characteristics and approaches that set them apart. Critical thinking is often described as convergent thinking; it involves a systematic process to arrive at a single, correct answer or solution to a specific problem. This approach relies heavily on logic, analysis, and evaluation of evidence, enabling individuals to sift through information and draw conclusions based on reasoned judgments.

In contrast, creative thinking is characterized by its divergent nature. This form of thinking encourages exploring multiple potential solutions or perspectives when faced with a problem. Creative thinkers embrace flexibility and originality, seeking innovative ideas that may not be immediately obvious. This process fosters an environment where brainstorming and open-ended inquiry can lead to novel discoveries and breakthroughs.

Understanding these fundamental differences is crucial for appreciating the unique contributions of each type of thinking. While critical thinking relies on accuracy and precision, creative thinking ventures into imagination and possibility, illustrating how individuals can approach challenges and generate solutions.

Looking at the details of critical and creative thinking, we see that critical thinking is objective and typically not influenced by personal feelings. In contrast, creative thinking is subjective and closely related to individual feelings, tastes, and opinions. Additionally, critical thinking is primarily associated with the left side of the brain, while creative thinking is linked to the right side. When a person practices critical thinking, they organize and analyze possibilities, using constructive thoughts and actions to explore the gathered information. Conversely, people who engage in creative thinking generate new connections based on unusual, original, and diverse ideas.

Although critical and creative thinking share similarities and differences, they are not mutually exclusive; instead, they complement each other. Critical thinkers use creativity to avoid biases and habit-formed conclusions, ensuring their thinking is objective and rational. Similarly, creativity uses critical thinking skills not to repeat what has been performed but to develop something new. As a result, it becomes evident that one entity cannot flourish or succeed without some manifestation of the other being present in its environment. Each relies on the other for existence and influence, creating a symbiotic relationship in which their growth and advancement are intertwined and mutually dependent.

What is your definition of *creativity*? Write it down so you can revisit and reflect on it.

How is *creativity* tied to critical thinking?

How has your *creativity* (or lack of) impacted your life up to this point?

How do critical thinking skills strengthen a person's sense of *creativity*?

Explain how developing a progressive sense of *creativity* can positively impact a person's life.

Explain how the absence of developing a sense of *creativity* may hurt a person's life. (For instance, avoiding potential dangers, understanding personal emotions, etc.)

Express how you feel about *creativity* being one of the most essential things in a successful life. (You may need to define the term successful.)

Chapter 11
Maximize Your Investments

A pessimist sees the difficulty in every opportunity; an optimist sees the opportunity in every difficulty.

— **Winston S. Churchill**

The effectiveness of advice depends on the recipient's willingness to act. Without implementation, the helpfulness of advice and shared experiences becomes little more than empty words. Many people may listen to advice and learn about others' struggles, but it ultimately serves little purpose if they do not act on that advice. Again, it is widely understood that quality advice can be transformative and immensely valuable. However, if someone with years of experience offers guidance, it will have no impact if the recipient does not put it into practice. Therefore, turning advice into action is the key.

Information shared in this chapter applies to various areas of life and is not limited to finances and education, which are the specific examples I will discuss. Furthermore, this chapter is designed for those who can immediately apply its advice, enabling them to take actionable steps after reading it.

However, readers who are unprepared to implement the suggestions may find the information useful but forget its significance if there is no immediate need to act on it. Given the importance of the book's concepts, I am sharing it with young adults who are receptive to its message, in hopes that they can use it immediately, and with those who are not ready to implement the concepts, can gain financial awareness, knowledge, and understanding to enhance their self-worth at a later time.

The concept of this chapter, 'maximizing your investments,' is not meant solely to focus on finances; however, since it is the first thing that comes to mind for most people, let's discuss it and create a framework for other life examples. If you have an IRA (individual retirement account), contribute each year when you can afford it. If you work for a large, well-established company that matches the money you save, save all you can. Invest in trusted stocks with a proven track record of growth and stability with every paycheck. It's okay if it is only a few dollars at a time.

Investing in your future can be one of the biggest challenges, but once you start, the only factor to consider is time. Allow time to grow your investment. You have already taken care of the most challenging aspect of investing for your future- getting started. Keeping your money invested will maximize your exposure to the financial market.

Save every allowable penny for that 'rainy day' in your future. Life should be an adventure filled with enjoyment, laughter, and memorable experiences. However, it's equally important to establish a financial savings plan that supports your future happiness and stability. You lay the groundwork for a more secure financial future by prioritizing saving over excessive spending.

Moreover, watching your savings grow over time can be immensely rewarding and will provide peace of mind when unexpected expenses arise. By adopting a saver's mindset, you invest in your financial security and build a safety net that lets you seize opportunities for enjoyment and adventure. Embrace the balance of living fully today while preparing for a brighter tomorrow.

When savers begin putting money away, they go through stages of struggle as they work toward financial success. The stages are considered obstacles that a person must overcome to reach higher levels of economic stability. In the early stages of saving, one (1) to five (5) years, the saver is aware of their money growing, and when it reaches an adequate level, they tend to take it out and buy something with it. They buy something they want as a 'thank you' to themselves for doing so well in saving money. This is a moment of pride, a reward for discipline and commitment. But, of course, they do not have the money anymore after making the purchase, and they start over from the beginning, saving their first dollar ($1) again.

Be cautious about letting small-ticket items and frivolous expenses, such as daily coffee runs, impulse buys, or frequent meals out, cloud your judgment of building substantial savings just because you can afford them. If this happens, adjust your saving goal to something much higher and continue saving. Don't fool yourself into thinking that saving is easy and that you can always start building up a hefty savings account whenever you want. Saving money should be considered problematic, so you will not waste your savings on small ticket items and purchases when you see them. When you consider saving as difficult, you will protect it from being traded for inconsequential things like buying a new gadget or eating out frequently.

Saving money is difficult because you will miss out on opportunities to buy items you think you need. Therefore, let trivial purchases pass you by and continue saving. Focus on saving for significant investments, such as a down payment for a home or a reliable car. By continuing to save and avoiding quick, easy opportunities to spend money, you will build peace of mind and see your money increase in value.

Through psychological behavior, comfort comes in many forms; one is the feeling of security. Stable finances will reduce anxiety about future financial independence and foster a sense of security. Worries about caring for yourself and supporting others who may rely on you will affect you less. The idea of losing your job, getting hurt, or not being able to work will seem less troublesome with a solid savings account. Hearing about the world going through its ups and downs and the chaos of this or that will seem less worrisome when you are financially secure. Allow this sense of security to motivate your continued efforts to save and invest in your future.

Having a solid financial plan and proactive steps to implement it provides reassurance that you have the resources to weather tough times or bounce back from setbacks. Therefore, keep your savings account growing by putting money aside whenever possible and maxing out your investments. In the words of William Arthur Ward, an

American writer, opportunities resemble sunrises in that, if you wait too long, you will miss them. With those words, this is a call to action, a reminder that the sooner you start saving, the sooner you will secure a more stable future.

As previously discussed, during the initial phase of saving money, which can span 1 to 5 years, you might find it challenging to resist purchasing small-ticket items. However, as you progress into the later stages, you'll start to see the fruits of your labor, having saved enough to invest in higher-quality items. By 'higher-quality' items, I refer to purchases that contribute to your long-term financial stability and overall well-being. Examples may include a home that increases in value, a dependable vehicle that transports you to work and helps you avoid costly repairs, or an investment that generates passive income.

Your financial mindset evolves in this later saving stage, which spans five (5) to ten (10) years or more. You begin to adopt an attitude that spending on unnecessary items feels less significant than before. By 'unnecessary,' I mean items that do not significantly contribute to your long-term financial security, such as luxury items, excessive vacations, or gifts to those who have not earned them and do not deserve them. Your thinking evolution changes from spending on unnecessary items to safeguarding your savings. I realized that every dollar you save and invest is a dollar you worked for. Your savings account represents your hard work.

Do not let your hard-earned savings go to waste. Good uses of saved resources include making a down payment on a home, investing in a stable dividend-paying stock, enrolling in higher education with a commitment to earn a degree to advance a career, etc. These moves are much wiser than locking it up in quickly depreciating assets such as a brand-new vehicle, a boat, excessive vacations, gambling, or personal loans. Purchasing new high-ticket items and spending on unnecessary things wastes resources. Thus, buying things that do not significantly enhance your financial security, such as expensive designer clothes, extended vacations, or giving your money away, will never build a large savings account needed to retire comfortably.

If you must spend money to keep your life progressing, keep in mind that buying a different or more reliable vehicle is a hundred times better than buying a 'brand-new' one. The basic idea of good transportation is captured by the phrase "reliable is reliable," and a lower-cost vehicle deemed reliable will perform the same function as an expensive one. The main advantage of purchasing a reliable, low-cost vehicle is that a significant portion of your money can stay in savings. Keep in mind that depreciating assets, like new cars and electronic gadgets, tend to lose value rapidly. Hence, your investment in them depreciates quickly.

In this later stage of savings, where you have amassed a substantial amount of money, the one item that can indeed pay off when you need it is a home. Although this concept can become complicated, the basic idea is that if you ever need extra cash, you can access more funds from a house through a second mortgage or a home equity line of credit than from depreciating assets. Therefore, it is advisable to purchase non-essential items much later in life when you have discretionary income. These available means are funds you can afford to spend without jeopardizing your financial security.

Let's discuss how to 'maximize your investment' in education. Paying for an education is not merely an expense; it's an investment in yourself that opens doors to better opportunities. A college degree and trade school experience broaden your horizons and expand your options for producing a stable future. However, if you're not interested in higher education (maxing out your educational experiences), at least earn a high school diploma. Statistics indicate that having a high school diploma significantly lowers the risk of legal troubles in adulthood. Evidence shows that 50% of individuals who do not graduate from high school encounter legal issues with the law and law enforcement at some point.

If you graduate from high school and do not think higher education is for you, acquire a trade or skill and learn all you can about it. The more education and knowledge you can receive about the trade you have chosen, the more job security you will give yourself. If becoming knowledgeable in your trade means taking a course or two at a college or trade school, I encourage you to do it. Taking one or two courses beyond what any other employee may do will put you ahead of others when it is time for a promotion. Doing this allows you to 'maximize' your educational experiences.

By now, it should be clear that investing in your education enhances your knowledge and skills and significantly boosts your self-worth and self-value. This commitment to personal development elevates your human capital, which represents your collective skills, knowledge, and experience. As you acquire new qualifications and expertise, you increase your attractiveness in the job market, open doors to more opportunities, and empower yourself to pursue higher levels of success. This investment lays a solid foundation for your professional growth and personal fulfillment, fostering a sense of confidence permeating all aspects of your life.

Even though earning a full degree and possibly a master's or doctorate would be considered 'maxing out' your potential, taking a few courses will show you are putting in some effort. A few courses in your field will show employers that you are willing to learn new things and recognize the importance of education in your job and self-improvement. In the words of Vince Lombardi, there is a price to success, and it comes through hard work, dedication, and determination in the face of winning or losing. His words reflect the importance of people applying themselves to their actions. Therefore, invest in your future by educating yourself in the area that interests you.

Building your financial stability and pursuing higher education enables you to take charge of your life, making your own decisions rather than relying on others. With this in mind, a key life goal is to empower yourself to take the reins of your choices. It's important to remember that relying on others to make decisions that you want to make a positive impact in your life is rare. Therefore, don't expect someone to come along and make transformative decisions for you better than you can for yourself. Keep pushing yourself to make the critical decisions that enhance your financial security, educational growth, and stronger relationships as you become self-reliant.

This brief chapter on making the most of your investments in finance and education also extends to your social circle, family, home, vehicle, and beyond. Maximizing your investments is about getting the best returns from your efforts and shaping your future according to your desires. Thus, taking the time today to establish what you'll need for tomorrow is an excellent first step toward building a stronger future.

Maximizing your friendships means staying connected, even if this means saying "hello" occasionally. Good friends are a treasure, and keeping them close is crucial. Maximizing your family time means avoiding arguments between you and them. You do not have to make it a mission to bring everyone together and live in harmony, but you can try, in small ways, to support the idea of what a supportive family looks like. Maximizing your home and vehicle means keeping them up to date with repairs so that more costly repairs will not surprise you later. A vehicle and a home are considered medium- to high-ticket items, and maximizing their efficiency by properly maintaining them is essential to ensuring they last a long time. I actively use this concept with my car. I have owned it for 25 years; it's my daily transportation, and I have nearly 370,000 miles on it. It almost looks new inside and out.

Unlocking your potential, whether through maximizing your learning or the usefulness of possessions, doesn't have to end there. By making the most of what you have, you can also help others maximize their resources. Being a proactive and considerate user can make a significant difference in others' lives. To help unlock the full potential of the homes you stay in and the vehicles you use, it's important to communicate any concerns you notice to the owner before they become more significant. If you are staying in a house with someone and borrowing a car, let those in charge know what has failed on it or is about to fail so they can make repairs and maximize their investment in their home or vehicle.

Not feeling obligated to tell the owner puts their investment at risk of more costly repairs. In retrospect, if you owned the home or car, you would want them to do the same for you. Therefore, let others know what is happening with what you are working with or using. Taking this approach will improve your ability to care for your belongings. By being mindful of others' needs, you also boost your sense of self-worth. Consequently, this mindset showcases your compassion and amplifies your ability to support those around you.

To reiterate a previous point, maximizing your investments can apply to many areas of life. It ultimately involves being aware of your surroundings and optimizing your resources. If you find your lack of higher education hinders your ability to enter the workforce at your desired capacity, consider changing your input toward education.

Enhance your learning potential by pursuing higher education or a trade school that interests you and aligns with a career you envision for yourself. If you lack security in your savings, find ways to cut costs. If you lack social involvement and it is important to you, join groups to maximize your social interactions.

Here is one final example that, while not directly related to finances or education, illustrates how maximizing your contributions can lead to personal growth. Note that a more developed version of yourself understands that compassion can enhance the efforts of others. Picture yourself walking through a supermarket and noticing a small puddle of water on the floor near the produce department.

This puddle, roughly the size of a washcloth, poses an apparent hazard, as it could easily cause someone to slip and fall. You promptly report the situation to an employee, who places a 'Wet Floor' sign over it. Before heading off to fetch a mop, the employee expressed appreciation, noting that if the spill had gone unnoticed and remained unaddressed, it could have led to a serious injury and exposed the store to potential financial liability.

Maximizing this situation can be understood as follows: Promptly cleaning up the spill prevents accidents and demonstrates the store's maximum commitment to customer safety. Additionally, it protects the overall investment in the health and well-being of individuals who may have been harmed, maximizing their protection. In both respects, you are maximizing your investment in caring for others.

Chapter 12
Less Negatives Mean More Positives

A constant stream of negative thoughts could easily become debilitating. But to become aware of those thoughts and to know that one's thoughts are not who they are, can be freeing.

—T.R. Ragan

Achieving a balanced life involves embracing both the positives and negatives we encounter. Positives often bring us joy and contribute to our overall well-being, while negatives represent distractions or obstacles that detract from a fulfilling life. Both positives and negatives can vary in significance, affecting our lives on large and small scales. The key takeaway is that by amplifying the positives, each person can shift the momentum toward leading a more satisfying life while simultaneously eliminating the negatives. Cultivating self-awareness and recognizing the difference between these two aspects of positives and negatives is crucial for personal growth.

Negativity in your life diminishes the impact of the positive things in your life. But if you drop a few negatives from your life, the positives will become stronger and more noticeable. For example, a negative could be a toxic relationship, a bad habit like procrastination, or a pessimistic outlook. By identifying and eliminating these negatives, you can enhance the positives. You should know that you are in control of this transformation, and it's a testament to your capability when you identify and dismiss the negatives.

My advice is simple: Don't worry about adding more positive things to your life. Adding more positives only gives the appearance of being in a better position. However, reducing the negatives will make a significant difference. Let's look at an example related to your health. Adding a longer or modified workout may help burn calories and support a better routine; however, the better course of action is reducing the unhealthy foods you consume. Eliminating poor diet choices would help a person stay healthier longer.

Adding more activity when there is already activity will not help as much as adjusting the kinds of foods you consume. This example of raising the positives (more time spent working out) but not lowering the negatives (limiting high-fat or low-energy foods) is a good example of doing more and getting less in return. A person would be much healthier by keeping the positives the same (their exercise routine) and eliminating the negatives (poor eating habits).

Consider this simple metaphor of adjusting the water temperature to illustrate how minimizing negatives can enhance the positives. Imagine hot water represents the things you desire, while cold water symbolizes the aspects you prefer to avoid. When setting the temperature for a shower and you want the water to feel hotter, you don't need to increase the hot water; instead, decrease the cold water. This adjustment will increase the ratio of hot to cold, making the water feel warmer. Similarly, you can make the positives more prominent by reducing the negatives in your life. This means you don't need to add more positive things to your life to feel better. You can do this by eliminating the negatives. Another example of improving the quality of life by reducing adverse events is a rushed routine. Rushed routines are driven by negative influences on outcomes. For example, driving faster and more aggressively to arrive at the next destination on time. From a driver's perspective, this is a 'positive' because they make it to their next destination on time or before. However, in reality, it's a 'negative' experience because they are not giving themselves enough time to get to their next destination and feel they need to be on time. Many of these negatives lead to poor outcomes, including increased stress and the potential for accidents.

They have increased the positive aspects (quickly moving from one point to another) without addressing the negatives (putting themselves in a rushed position and others in a compromising situation). This person would fare better by keeping the positives the same (driving the posted speed limit) and finding ways to lessen the negatives (giving themselves more time). Many situations in life would improve if people focused on removing negatives rather than continually seeking to add positives. The positives grow heavier as you drop the negativity.

A way to lessen the negatives in this scenario is to set an appointment alarm earlier than usual to allow more time to drive from point A to point B. Another would be to check the alarm to ensure it is set correctly and goes off as intended.

Confirming that these negative events do not happen is reassuring, as it makes the positives more likely to occur.

Here is another way to accentuate the positives as you head out for the day. As you prepare to leave your home and think about additional tasks to take care of before you leave for your destination, let them go. Don't allow yourself to get sidetracked. Make a point to leave on time. Drop the negatives that will interfere with your intended plans and let the positives become stronger.

Let's use school as an example of increasing the positives by reducing the negatives when completing assignments and studying for tests. The positives are putting in worthwhile studying for quizzes and tests, and submitting assignments on time. Thus, you can view the positives as the accumulated knowledge gained and your dedication. Doing what is required of you, or at least attempting to have a genuine intention to accomplish things, is a positive. These positives are a testament to your hard work and dedication.

Conversely, the negatives that counter the positives are the moments that pull you away from work. These moments include refusing to engage in any assignment, doing things to avoid having time to complete your work, or thinking assignments do not matter to your overall education. In essence, the 'negatives' are the times you could have put into studying and did not.

One effective way to curb the negatives is to set aside a dedicated block of time for it during the day. Consider allocating a specific period, like 30 minutes in the evening, while reserving the rest of the day for productive tasks (positives). This approach maximizes the benefits of staying engaged in work, completing assignments, and studying for exams while confining procrastination's downsides (negatives) to a limited timeframe.

Do not allow yourself unlimited free time to do whatever comes your way. This is when negatives begin to outweigh the positives and interfere with obligations. Although you may have plenty of free moments, filling them with unproductive activities, such as mindless scrolling on social media or binge-watching television programs, often leads to more negative moments than positives. The negative will overshadow the positive, creating a stressful situation.

Besides prioritizing your free time, you can increase the positives to outweigh the negatives in simple ways. One practical approach is to be actively engaged and attentive in settings such as the classroom, the workplace, or important meetings. While you remain focused, consider taking notes if it helps you stay focused. You can later reflect on these notes when studying for quizzes, tests, or the tasks you are responsible for at work. Ultimately, reducing the negatives hinges on your engagement and will require some effort on your part.

Eliminating the negatives will not be easy initially, but consistent effort will improve the ratio of negatives to positives. Lowering the number of negative events will increase the ratio of positive events, thereby boosting your potential for engagement and success. This concept of reducing the negative and raising the positive can be applied to every area of life. It can apply to friendships by avoiding confrontations (negatives) so that the good times are more frequent (positives). You can use it at work by not being late (negative), so that others see you as someone who cares about the place you work (positive).

Keep in mind that there are only a limited number of moments in each day, so it's important to make the most of your time. Before you know it, a year will have passed, and if you haven't addressed some negative aspects of your life to highlight the positives, you'll find yourself in the same position as the previous year. You want to avoid a year passing without making things better. Therefore, eliminating just one ongoing significant adverse event can increase your chances of success.

Switching gears but staying on topic, it's essential to recognize that life can only be so full. This is because everything we engage in requires time. Even the hours we spend sleeping will be deducted from the 24 hours we have each day. No one can have more hours than anyone else; everyone is limited to 24 hours. At its core, this involves simply adding and subtracting. However, how we, or you, decide to spend that time is entirely open to interpretation.

If you spend most of your time sleeping, you will have the remaining hours available for other activities, such as socializing with friends and family, working, or pursuing hobbies. Conversely, if you dedicate many hours to work, you can use the leftover time to sleep or connect with friends. Finding a balance in how you allocate your 24 hours is essential, as it helps you feel reassured and guided in your daily life.

I advise reducing the time spent on negative things, such as toxic relationships and unhealthy habits. Unhealthy habits can range from smoking to excessive screen time to unproductive routines like procrastination or lack of exercise. By lowering the time spent on these and other negatives, the positives, such as self-care, meaningful relationships, and personal growth, become more meaningful and valuable. The best route to making a positive difference is to eliminate the negatives.

However, if you take a different route by adding more positives to offset the negatives, the number of negatives remains the same. Thus, there will be no overall improvement. Therefore, it is more beneficial to eliminate the negative things that weigh you down and hold you back than to add more positives. Furthermore, adding more positives may seem like the better choice, but it will complicate your life. What will happen is that the positives you add will turn into negatives because you cannot use them as intended. Consequently, this will add more negatives to your life.

The best option is to eliminate the existing negatives to accentuate the remaining positives. Additionally, the more positive things you have, the less room there will be for trivial and adverse things. Consequently, the more time you spend doing good things, the less time you have for bad things to take root and develop. This is what I mean by a 'balancing act.' It's about consciously investing your time and energy in positive activities that increase your self-worth, reducing the space for negative influences.

It's crucial to understand that you don't need to increase the positive aspects of your life to see a change; simply letting go of some harmful elements that have become a part of your routine can bring relief. Don't allow these harmful elements to consume any more of your time. Cease engaging in some of the negative habits that counter the positives. For example, if you're a smoker, quitting is a way to eliminate a negative influence. If you want a healthier lifestyle, you don't have to take up jogging longer distances or working out harder as an added positive; just stop smoking. This way, you free yourself from harmful habits and enhance the positives that are already in your life.

If you find yourself staying up too late and, as a result, regularly sleeping through your alarm, it's time to eliminate the negative influence of staying up. You don't need to add more positives, such as finding a louder alarm to help you wake up on time; just reduce the negatives by going to bed at a reasonable hour before you become too tired to manage your necessary morning routine. By lessening the negative influence, you create a more peaceful and balanced life where the positives naturally thrive.

I will leave you with a final example. It concerns finances and acquired debt. Too much debt is like a bad habit; it starts small and builds to a point that is difficult to manage or control. Since people often want to show their best side, they usually add things to their lives (which push them into debt). In retrospect, their lives appear balanced to their friends and neighbors, but they have increased the negatives (debt). Their lifestyles have been enhanced by buying nicer cars, going on vacations, eating out regularly, and buying the latest gadgets. They add these things by using credit. Hence, they have added a negative to their life and not a positive as it might appear.

Furthermore, many people who have taken on debt stay late at work or take on a part-time job to earn extra money to pay for the toys they bought on credit. Unfortunately, poor financial habits that lead to increased debt don't improve simply by earning more money. Often, the income-to-debt ratio deteriorates over time because individuals tend to buy more as their income rises. While it may seem optimistic that money is coming in from the additional work, this can be detrimental. People in this situation work longer and harder to pay for items they don't have the free time to enjoy.

A more effective approach would be to cut back on some negatives, particularly by reducing the number of unnecessary items they feel compelled to finance. By letting go of these extras, individuals can improve their outlook on life, as they won't have to work as hard to pay for things they don't truly need or have the time to enjoy. As these burdens diminish, they can scale back their extra work hours and focus on the positive aspects that truly matter. Removing the negatives can naturally increase the positives.

Critical Thinking and Self-esteem

Self-esteem is defined as confidence in one's abilities and is closely linked to self-worth. It encompasses a person's ideals and beliefs about themselves, as well as their emotional states, including feelings of despair or triumph. In psychology, self-esteem is considered a vital indicator of mental health. Thus, various factors influence an individual's self-esteem, including thoughts, feelings, and life experiences.

Generally, self-esteem is a person's positive or negative feelings about themselves. It's how people feel about their abilities and their place in the world. Self-worth, however, is the value we place on ourselves, regardless of our actions or circumstances. It's the belief that one deserves respect and love, irrespective of achievements or failures. Self-esteem and self-worth are closely linked to critical thinking, as individuals assess their value and consider their contributions to the world around them. Therefore, critical thinking is vital in establishing a solid sense of 'self' and contributes to the building blocks of sound self-esteem.

Besides a person's ability to think critically and the skills they possess to rationalize their thoughts in needed situations, many factors affecting self-esteem vary across cultures. For instance, in some cultures, individual achievement is highly valued, which can lead to higher self-esteem in those who excel. In contrast, some cultures value collective harmony, which can lead to higher self-esteem among those who contribute to a group or organization. Consequently, understanding cultural nuances is essential to comprehending the broader concept of self-esteem.

Numerous studies have demonstrated that self-esteem and critical thinking are distinct concepts. However, they are meaningfully interconnected. Critical thinking helps individuals gain confidence in navigating life's challenges, regardless of background or circumstances. Thus, to improve oneself and make positive personal changes, it is essential to have the desire to grow. This is where self-esteem plays a vital role, as it is influenced by factors that can differ from person to person as they navigate life's challenges.

In one study, the researchers used correlation analysis to examine relationships among various personality traits and self-esteem. It revealed that several characteristics, including analytical thinking, open-mindedness, curiosity, confidence, and truth-seeking, were significantly correlated with self-esteem. Notably, open-mindedness and curiosity emerged as strong predictors of self-esteem. Thus, individuals can dramatically enhance their self-esteem by cultivating these traits and promoting personal development.

While further research is needed to grasp the impact of critical thinking on self-esteem, one thing is sure: you can shape your self-esteem through critical thinking. For example, when you receive negative feedback, take the time to evaluate it critically rather than just accepting it at face value, and don't let it dishearten you. Understanding this relationship to assess incoming information empowers you to take control of your self-worth, because no one can make you feel a way you do not want to. Therefore, implement critical thinking skills to enhance your self-esteem, as you are the best person to manage your life. You need to be the architect of your life and the gatekeeper of how you feel and respond to situations, regardless of how others act.

Cultivating and applying critical thinking skills is vital for making informed decisions. Conversely, failing to develop or use these skills can lead to poor judgment. Therefore, it's important to avoid mimicking the behavior of those who act without thinking. Thus, start thinking for yourself, even if it means distancing yourself from friends who undermine your self-esteem and promote unwise choices.

Cultivating critical thinking skills equips you to analyze and evaluate information beyond the immediate influence of your emotions, feelings, and actions. This cognitive process enables you to navigate challenges and make informed, independent decisions, fostering a sense of autonomy essential to personal growth. As you enhance your critical thinking abilities, you build confidence in your decision-making and develop a deepened sense of self-reliance. This empowerment contributes to a richer understanding of your values and beliefs, reinforcing your self-worth and promoting resilience in the face of adversity.

What is your definition of *self-esteem*? Write clearly and concisely here:

How is *self-esteem* tied to critical thinking?

How has your *self-esteem* (or lack of) impacted your life up to this point?

How do critical thinking skills strengthen a person's sense of *self-esteem*?

Explain how developing a progressive sense of *self-esteem* can positively impact a person's life.

Explain how the absence of developing a sense of *self-esteem* may hurt a person's life. (For instance, avoiding potential dangers, understanding personal emotions, etc.)

Express how you feel about *self-esteem* being one of the most essential things in a successful life. (You may need to define the term successful.)

Chapter 13
Not Created or Destroyed, Only Changed

In nature, nothing is created, and nothing is destroyed, but everything is transformed

— **Antoine Laurent Delavosier**

We often take what we use daily for granted and don't think about its origin. It may be challenging to grasp at first, but everything manufactured ultimately comes from the Earth, meaning everything you have ever used has its roots in natural resources. Aluminum, steel, and plastics found in various modes of transportation—such as cars, trains, buses, airplanes, and boats—are all derived from the Earth. Aluminum is produced from excavated bauxite rock, mined in hundreds of millions of tons, while steel is created by combining iron ore with oxygen and other minerals.

Paved roads on highways and freeways worldwide are primarily made of asphalt and concrete, a combination of bitumen (an oil-based substance) and crushed rock and sand. Minerals were extracted and used to make plastics and rubber compounds for the buildings we work in, the arenas where we play sports, and the packaging for the food we purchase. Man created every piece of plastic on Earth based on understanding polymers in the natural world. All the world's Tupperware and everything that has ever come wrapped in plastic deviated from the Earth.

Plants have been harvested and extensively studied for their medicinal properties, leading to the development of various medicines and medical devices that promote health and wellness. Researchers examine the active compounds found in these botanical sources, such as alkaloids, flavonoids, and terpenoids, which have demonstrated effectiveness in treating various ailments. Medical advancements, including plant-derived antibiotics, anti-inflammatory agents, and natural supplements, underscore the significance of botanical research in contemporary medicine. Man did not create the essence of these plants; they were only harvested, synthesized, and changed into what we use them for today.

The Earth has provided the materials and resources, such as lumber and concrete, for the places we call home and the buildings we work in. Our clothes result from manipulating cotton in textile machines and manufacturing fibers like synthetic polyester derived from petroleum. Additionally, all the food anyone has ever eaten has come from the Earth. This has grown the world population to over 8,000,000,000 people in 2025, and the number continues to increase by roughly 70 million each year.

There is nothing on this Earth that was brought here from another planet and used to help support humanity and civilization. Everything used to make what we have today originated here on Earth in a different form. Nothing has been created or destroyed; it has just changed its structure. Kids might believe everything appears on the store shelves, but we know that isn't quite the whole story. We understand that the items we purchase are made from various materials. For instance, books aren't just found on shelves; a book's final product starts with the hard work of chopping down trees and hauling them away, turning them into pulp, then into paper, and eventually into paper that can be written on. There's an entire process behind how everything in our world has come to be as we see it today.

Resource transformation is often a one-way journey. The materials used to create items do not revert to their original form. For instance, when heated to high temperatures, sand, soda ash, and limestone melt into a clear liquid. These liquid glass forms, upon cooling, are used in applications such as car windshields, home windows, storefronts, and mirrors. If glass were to shatter, it would not return to its original form (sand, soda, and ash); it would not disappear or leave the planet. It would turn into a resource for other applications. Glass, much like various products shaped by human ingenuity, turns raw materials into everyday items that profoundly affect our lives.

The review of natural resources above being turned into other usable products is an analogy for young adults' vital role in changing the world around them. As a young adult, you are not just a passive consumer but an active participant. You have the power to influence cultures, societies, and environments worldwide. This power is inherent within you and must be cultivated to bring about meaningful change. You have the resources within you to make a difference in the world; you only need to develop them into tools to make the changes. Furthermore, it is crucial to recognize that everyone plays a vital role in this transformation process.

Unfortunately, limited perspectives and self-centered lifestyles often focus solely on tangible items consumed rather than on the inherent value of the resources everyone possesses to change their lives. A broader and more passionate view reveals that everything is transformative. Your time and energy are transformative in completing goals. Your everyday experiences are transformed into new perspectives and understandings. As Jillian Michaels, an American businesswoman, aptly puts it, transformation occurs in the present through movement, and it is our responsibility to manage this transformation wisely.

Acquiring an education is one of the most powerful tools a young adult has for transformation. It equips them with knowledge and skills and shapes their character, values, and aspirations, preparing them to navigate the complexities of the modern world. Speaking directly to you, education is about learning truths, generating perspectives, influencing, and being influenced by various understandings. With a strong knowledge base and prior experience, you can become a well-rounded individual who can navigate societies and cultures, making valuable contributions.

Your aptitude and desire are intrinsic qualities that do not require fabrication; they are inherent traits that you already have, much like the abundant resources on Earth. Just as we cannot generate additional resources or wholly eliminate them from the Earth, these qualities remain a constant part of your essence. However, just like natural resources can be transformed into various tools and technologies that enhance our quality of life, your innate abilities and passions can be harnessed and refined to construct the identity you aspire to embody. With intentional focus and development, these attributes can be shaped into powerful tools that facilitate your journey.

As a young adult, consider yourself in a transformative light: you develop as you gather, combine, and implement different resources within and around you. You have immense potential for greatness within you, a power that can achieve extraordinary things. You can either remove obstacles from your path or use them as stepping-stones to reach greater heights. You possess the mental strength to create new dreams and the discipline to make them a reality. Remember that transformation is not only a tangible and external process but must also occur within you. You have all the tools you need to succeed; therefore, you must combine your internal resources with external actions to change your life.

During your formative years, you accumulate information and learn to process and apply it. This is not just a period of transformation in your life, but a crucial phase where your efforts shape your future. The decisions you make and the knowledge you acquire in your academic years will significantly impact your future path. Education is a powerful tool that can open doors to a world of opportunities. Thus, school is not just a stepping-stone into the adult world, a more mature world, but a foundation for the life you want to build. Your choices at this time in your life will reverberate throughout your life, so choose wisely and work diligently.

Connecting these two concepts of Earth resources changed into beneficial products we use, and your attributes harnessed into beneficial tools you use, we see that nothing is created or destroyed, only changed to support a better way of life. Excavators and scientists have transformed natural materials, such as ore into steel, bauxite into aluminum, and sand into glass. Similarly, you have been working to enhance your critical thinking skills by processing information from your life experiences and educational courses. The elements of the Earth have shaped the societies we live in and everything we use. In the same way, you have the potential to influence how society evolves by applying your critical thinking abilities.

The things you aspire to achieve and the people you choose to emulate are not just distant dreams but reality already existing within you. By engaging in your education, you are shaping your raw potential and transforming it into the dreams you wish to fulfill. Just as the Earth's raw materials are turned into items that benefit our lives, you can convert the knowledge you acquire into everything you want to become. Everything you wish to be is already inside you, just in a different form. You may need to refine your skills through additional studying and a few more years of discipline, but you already have all the elements to achieve greatness.

Consider your secondary and formal education as an opportunity to explore your interests and talents, fostering personal growth and fulfillment. Make this period in your life about learning and self-discovery. The more knowledge you acquire in school and beyond, the more resources you will have to build stronger and more fulfilling dreams. All you need to do is transform the knowledge you gain into various aspects of your aspirations. Everything you need to achieve greatness is already within you, just like the wonderful things we use today were transformed from the Earth.

All the fantastic things you use today (vehicles, homes, technology, etc.) that make your life easier and more manageable come from the Earth. The resources to make these items were on this planet millions of years ago, just in a different form- a non-realized form. It was the desire to want a better life, the struggle to gather them from deep in the Earth, the energy to break them down, the ingenuity to see their potential, and the scientific minds to combine them that have formed them into their new existence.

Recognizing the impact of determined leaders who transformed materials into essential modern tools and luxuries we use today, you should strive to excel during your young adult years by using the resources available and within you. The more knowledge you acquire, the better equipped you will be to shape your life and achieve your goals. In a moment of pause and critical thinking, you should realize that your desire and effort are the only things that separate the resources within you from your actual achievements.

Your skills, knowledge, attributes, and personal qualities are these resources within you. You need to pull these resources together, reach out to others for help and guidance, and put in the time and energy to make your dreams happen. Now, in your young adult life, is the time to search for and gather resources to build a better life. Conversely, suppose you do not intentionally invest in your young adult life by failing to develop the resources within you into something more meaningful. In that case, you will lack the tools and structure necessary to sustain a productive future, leading to a life that heavily relies on others. Do not allow your resources to sit idle inside you while your life advances.

Your teachers, counselors, and other mentors are here to help you identify and utilize your resources. Focus your early years on meaningful pursuits for maximum productivity. Every day is an opportunity to make good decisions that will shape your future. By making intelligent, sensible choices, you can avoid wasting resources and the need to redo your efforts. Backtracking to clean up or repair mistakes wastes time and energy and does not put the resources you have gathered and synthesized to good use.

Revisiting past mistakes to make corrections can waste valuable time. Nobody wants to repeat things they do not have to. There is no point in going back to redo something that could have been done correctly, or better, the first time. Using your knowledge and drive to earn an educational degree is an example of how to apply your resources (time, money, effort) to earn good grades, pass courses, and graduate into a career that will allow you to live a fulfilling life. However, retaking courses multiple times because you are failing them is not a good use of resources. As you can see, revisiting past events or obstacles to redo them or make corrections can waste valuable time.

Another example of using your resources wisely is abiding by society's laws and rules; doing so will help you move through life more easily than if you break the law. Failing to live by some important law can land you in jail or prison. Both of which are forms of paying restitution for your poor choices. Paying restitution for past poor decisions will not easily advance you through life or foster personal growth. When poor choices keep happening, it is like burning your resources; no tangible good comes of it.

In summary, everything we use today was already in this world but has merely changed form. Likewise, you possess all the resources within you to transform into a stronger, more independent person. The only thing missing is your desire to change your resources into fulfilled dreams. These internal resources need to be reshaped, and you can achieve this by making wise choices. You only need to act.

Chapter 14
Believe You Are Enough

No one can make you feel inferior without your consent.

— **Eleanor Roosevelt**

There is no one else in the world exactly like you. You are a unique individual with distinct abilities, talents, and gifts. These abilities and gifts include your capacity for deep empathy, problem-solving, and a knack for making others laugh. While some people may look, act, talk, or walk similarly, they do not share your specific mannerisms, personality, or thoughts. This uniqueness stems from your individual experiences and the way you interpret them. As we all know, countless small events occur daily, and you perceive and react to them in your own way.

You will experience emotions about specific events in a unique way and articulate your thoughts about them in ways no one else does. You are not only unique; you are irreplaceable. No one in the world can take your place or replicate your unique facial expressions, tone of voice, or cadence. The events you've experienced and expressed have shaped you into a one-of-a-kind individual. Furthermore, your interactions and connections with others have left an indelible mark, making you unique.

Remember that you are enough, and everything you do, no matter how small, makes a significant difference. Therefore, make decisions that serve your best interests and foster your growth. Embrace courage when making decisions. This will bolster your own bravery and inspire and uplift those around you. Know that your words make a difference and impact others. Your viewpoints and expressions are stamped with your personality. You don't need anything else in your life to complete you. You don't need anything added to your life to make you feel worthy of other people's views about yourself. You already have it within you; you are enough.

It has to be enough because nobody else can replace you. For this reason, don't allow anyone to take your place or your voice. Care for yourself enough to know that you have value. Your opinion matters, your thoughts matter, and your physical self matters. For instance, if you have a unique perspective on a topic, it's not just important; it's invaluable. Share it with others. Don't allow others to speak for you if you want to share. You need to speak up and speak out to show yourself that you matter.

Take the initiative to speak up and be heard on important issues in your life. Speak up if you believe your input will help others. Do not hand over control of your feelings to others; do not allow them to speak your thoughts for you. Do not allow yourself to fall into the trap of allowing others to validate your feelings and try to express them for you. Allowing others to express your feelings gives them too much power in your life. You must retain your power since you are unique and have thoughts and feelings nobody can express with your specific rhythm and tone.

The power you hold in being an individual is a wonderful thing. It should be protected and encouraged. However, when giving up your power to express yourself, you hand over the 'keys' of your individuality to someone else. These 'keys' represent your unique voice, ability to express your thoughts and feelings, and power to shape your narrative. Don't let others hold the keys to your sense of validation. You alone need to possess these keys that affirm your worth and remind you that you make a significant difference.

The power of your words and how you express them is incredibly significant, and keeping that power for yourself is vital. Never allow anyone else to control your sense of self-worth—only you should determine that you are enough and that what you say and do truly matters. Embrace the strength in your voice and the impact of your actions, and always remember that you are the keeper of your validation.

When allowing others to speak your voice, especially at crucial times in your life, you give up a little of your self-validation. Self-validation is recognizing and accepting your thoughts, feelings, and values as important and valid. Validation is understanding that your unique perspective and experiences are valuable and should be considered relevant. When you speak up about issues that matter to you and could impact your life, you are not just expressing yourself; you are actively changing your life in ways that you see as relevant.

Do not underestimate your power as an individual or allow others to overlook you when validating issues that directly concern you. Allowing others to speak on your behalf about what you can express yourself means accepting their version of your intelligence, beauty, and impact. You are granting them the authority to shape your self-perception and how you see yourself. This harms you, as it gives others control over your self-expression. It also gives others the ability to silence you. Being silenced means you have little impact on your life and those you hope to change.

Relying on others to voice your thoughts might feel comfortable at first, but over time, it can lead you to adopt their views as your own. When this happens, you seek validation from others about how you feel regarding yourself and the world around you, rather than looking within for those perspectives. You will find yourself waiting on others around you, to whom you gave the 'voice keys,' to confirm how you feel about yourself. Again, when this happens, you lose your power as an individual and instead wait for others to confirm what you have the right to feel and express on your own.

Not owning your voice can lead to believing you are not enough. You place your self-worth in their hands by giving others the power to validate you. You are making their opinions about you more significant than your view of yourself. To regain control, start by acknowledging your thoughts and feelings, then express them without seeking validation from others. This could involve journaling, using positive affirmations, or simply reminding yourself daily of your unique abilities and self-worth. Mindfulness and self-reflection can also help you better understand and appreciate your unique thoughts and feelings.

Receiving compliments about your terrific qualities can feel nice. However, do not let others' opinions or compliments dictate how you feel about yourself. Compliments are nice and welcome, but they are external validations, and when you rely on them or seek them from others, you put yourself in a needy position, which is not a good place to be. Instead, focus on internal validation, which comes from within and is based on your perception of self-worth and self-acceptance. You should always retain the voice that speaks to you about your self-esteem, self-reliance, and self-actualization. It is your way of maintaining control over how you want to feel and when you want to feel it.

In times of disappointment and sadness, remember that you have the sole ownership and ultimate power to make yourself feel how you want. If you feel sad in good times, know it's because you've made that choice. If you feel good in bad times, know it's because you've made that choice. You are the deciding factor in how you think, why you feel, and when you feel it. Do not allow others to manipulate how, why, and when you think about anything. Allowing this to happen gives others too much power over your freedoms.

Allowing others to dictate these occasions and responses will not increase your individual growth. Therefore, taking hold of them will testify to your resilience and strength. Nobody should be able to make you feel the way you do not want to, and nobody should have power over your emotions and feelings. By allowing others to hold the 'keys' to your emotions and feelings, you will rely on their validation to make you feel better in bad times and accept their words, which can make you feel worse in good times. You don't need this; therefore, believe you are enough.

It is well known that certain people have unique support systems that others do not. For this reason, there is an unfair playing field when it comes to emotional stability. There is also an unfair playing field when it comes to confidence in one's abilities. Some may have strong support systems that have encouraged them their entire lives, while others did not. This can make a lot of difference in how a person sees themselves and how they can self-manage and work through events in their life. If you do not have a positive support system (one, two, or three close friends) to encourage you, then you need to seek out those who can help you build your inner voice. However, do not seek out 'friends' who speak 'for you' but those who allow you to speak 'for yourself.'

The last comment in this chapter is about being yourself and not wanting to be anyone else. Your voice makes a difference, and you should want to be you. If you do not want to be you but instead someone else, who will take your place? If this happens, the world will be without your unique voice. On the other hand, suppose you could be someone else who has made a good life for themselves. In that case, it would not be fair of you to want only a part of their exciting life and not their entire life.

Being someone else because you see a portion of their life is not a valid argument. If you see the glitz and glamour of another person's life and wish you were them, having only the best of what you know about them would not be possible. You cannot take the singular parts of their life without all the prior things that contributed to making them who they are. Wanting a part of someone's life is not fair to your subconscious; therefore, you have to want their entire life to set yourself free from desiring their life. Wanting only parts of their life is a subconscious fantasy.

Forcing yourself to look at their entire life and choose it over your own will help you free yourself from wanting parts of it. For example, people think about wanting what others drive, wear, or live in. But people who want these things lie to themselves because they do not see the cost of owning them or the burden they entail. Consequently, it is not fair to one's mind to want the parts of other people's lives without wanting all that comes with them.

If you stop to think about it, and then tell yourself you want every aspect of someone else's life—their good and bad moments from the moment they were born until you decide to become them—you will soon realize that you don't truly desire all of it. In other words, if you attempt to immerse yourself in every facet of someone else's existence—embracing not only their joyous milestones but also their struggles, heartbreaks, and hardships, stretching from the day they entered the world to the instant you choose to inhabit their shoes—you will come to a deep actualization: the entirety of their journey, with all its complexities, is not something you genuinely long for.

While you may admire certain aspects of their lives, the weight of their challenges, vulnerabilities, and experiences is often far more burdensome than it appears from the outside. Coming to this understanding reveals a profound truth about desire and identity; it highlights the importance of cherishing your own unique path rather than coveting another's.

This recognition that you cannot pick and choose from another person's life will help you understand that your life is what you want. You'll quickly see that you have grown attached to your memories and comfortable routines, which are hard to let go of. You will soon realize that relinquishing all your memories to take on someone else's life is not what you truly want. You will also understand that what you desired from the other person was merely the superficial aspects of their life.

Instead of longing for what others have, focus on creating the life you want by committing to expressing your authentic voice. Believe that you are good enough and that your voice can help you achieve anything you desire. There is no need to covet what others possess. Your voice and actions can make the life you want.

Before we wrap up, I want to share one last idea. Think of time and distance as ways to help you get things done. They can level the playing field, shaping how we see things and how we act. Often, what sets people apart is not ability, but how they look at a situation.

Take distance as an example. If someone excels at a task from where they stand and you can’t replicate it, the issue may not be skill—it may be position. Move closer, and the details come into focus, helping you match their accuracy. Step back, and the broader pattern becomes visible.

It's the same idea behind the saying that you can't see the forest for the trees. Up close, you notice individual details but lose sight of the whole. From farther away, you see the full landscape but miss the finer points. Each perspective offers something different—and necessary.

Time works in a similar way, but instead of changing perspective, it changes opportunity. Sometimes the difference between success and failure isn't skill—it's timing. Move too fast, and you miss important steps. Move too slowly, and opportunities pass you by.

It's like driving on the freeway. If you need to make an exit, you may have to speed up to get ahead of traffic or slow down to fall in behind it. Either way, adjusting your timing puts you in the right position to succeed.

Ultimately, both time and distance are tools we can adjust to better understand situations and improve our outcomes. By being intentional about our perspective and timing, we can bridge skill or performance gaps and put ourselves in the best position to succeed.

Critical Thinking and Fairness

Many similar words often get intertwined, leading to confusion about their meanings. Two such words are 'fairness' and 'friendly.' Being fair does not always mean being friendly. Fairness involves making just and equitable decisions by considering all relevant factors and perspectives; therefore, being friendly may not always apply. In contrast, being friendly during a negotiation can result in an unfair compromise. Thus, being friendly may not always incorporate fairness.

Consider a scenario in which a negotiator's friendliness leads to a verdict not in their party's best interest, such as agreeing to a higher price than necessary or to unfavorable conditions for the other party. While 'friendly' can foster a suitable relationship between parties, it should not overshadow fairness. In such a situation, a 'friendly' compromise may not be fair to all parties, as being friendly does not equate to being equitable.

Many see and experience fairness differently, but it fundamentally serves everyone's best interest. However, achieving a fair and equitable balance is a significant challenge. It can be helpful to consider that fairness is more closely related to truthfulness and honesty than friendliness. This is because fairness is strongly associated with equity. Moreover, fairness is linked to ethics in prioritizing the interests of all parties involved rather than merely being friendly.

While people may not always agree with verdicts and outcomes, the commitment to fairness ensures that everyone's needs and perspectives are considered before a conclusion is reached. Linking critical thinking to fairness, we see it as essential in pursuing fairness, as it helps define the boundaries of what is fair. By emphasizing the importance of critical thinking in achieving fairness, individuals are empowered to take responsibility for the fairness of their decisions and actions.

It's important to note that critical thinking should not be devoid of empathy, the ability to understand and share others' feelings. This point is crucial in conclusions as it considers perspectives and can balance fairness. Emphasizing empathy not only helps all parties feel more connected to the decision-making process but also ensures that their feelings are understood and considered. When applied correctly, critical thinking with empathy ensures that outcomes are not one-sided or skewed. This is because critical thinking, like fairness, is impartial.

Our empathy, integrated with critical thinking, helps us consider how our choices affect others and adjust our approach accordingly. This ensures everyone's needs are considered. It does not favor one side over the other due to personal bias; instead, it analyzes the information and considers the feelings of all parties to arrive at the best conclusion. This impartiality of critical thinking, combined with empathy and fairness, provides security and confidence in decision-making, ensuring that all parties can trust its objectivity.

The ultimate goal of fairness is to achieve balance and compromise when addressing issues and resolving conflicts. In workplace conflicts, fairness involves giving equal consideration to all parties' perspectives. This focus on balance and compromise reassures everyone that the process is fair and helps instill confidence in the resolution. However, achieving this balance can be challenging, especially when personal biases or external pressures are at play. Ultimately, fairness acts as a standard for monitoring and balancing solutions and outcomes.

The art of fairness enables individuals to reflect on what is reasonable and to return to the principles of justice. This critical thinking skill, which involves continually reassessing what is fair, is a hallmark of those with a high level of cognitive awareness. People who consistently seek common ground, ensuring that both sides receive what they deserve based on their contributions, exemplify critical thinking. Thus, critically analyzing issues and striving for the best solution without bias is inherently connected to fairness.

Making persuasive arguments and using colorful language will not easily influence those committed to thinking critically about fair outcomes. Critical thinkers can recognize when rhetoric distracts from logic and tries to convince others of arguments that are uneven or unbalanced. Critical thinking is firmly grounded in the basics of fairness, which means treating all relevant viewpoints equally, regardless of an individual's feelings or interests. Consequently, every perspective is respected and considered when pursuing fairness, even when personal biases exist. This approach serves as the foundation and boundaries of critical thinking.

Furthermore, committing to fairness ensures that decisions are not swayed by personal bias but guided by a sense of responsibility to treat all viewpoints equally. Given that people tend to be biased in their perspectives, it becomes even more imperative to maintain the intellectual standard of fairness at the forefront of our minds. Therefore, it is beneficial to develop critical thinking skills to assist in decisions that require fairness.

What is your definition of *fairness*? Write it down so you can revisit and reflect on it.

How is *fairness* tied to critical thinking?

How has your sense of *fairness* (or lack of) impacted your life up to this point?

How do critical thinking skills strengthen a person's sense of *fairness*?

Take a moment to think, then share an event or a time in your life when *fairness* came to the forefront of your actions or thoughts.

Explain how developing a progressive sense of f*airness* can positively impact a person's life.

Explain how the absence of developing a sense of *fairness* may hurt a person's life. (For instance, avoiding potential dangers, understanding personal emotions, etc.)

Express how you feel about *fairness* being one of the most essential things in a successful life. (You may need to define the term successful.)

Chapter 15
Keep Going Until Failure Fades

Practice to the point of getting it right is only the initial phase of being successful. Thus, practice until failing ceases to exist.

— **Douglas Allan Portello**

Failure is an intriguing phenomenon; it is often inconsistent and unpredictable. Failure happens even when the odds of a positive outcome are in our favor. There is no formula to foresee it coming, as it can occur in countless ways, just as there are many ways to avoid it. Therefore, failure should not be seen as the end. Instead, it should serve as a test of resilience and the ability to adapt and bounce back.

Failure, in this chapter's context, refers to events whose outcomes can be altered through discipline. Therefore, overcoming failure lies in our hands and the power of practice. By overcoming challenges, we can acknowledge our strengths and guide our adaptability. Thus, while failure may occur, we have the power to minimize its impact through intentional and purposeful practice.

Suppose you are playing an individual sport, such as tennis or paddleball, and playing amazingly well. It is still possible to lose. You probably heard the expression, 'Failure is not an option.' Well, it is. It is always an option. Talented professional tennis players can return a tennis ball served at them at over 120mph with perfect form and still not get the ball back into play. Unaccounted variables may cause the ball to go slightly out of bounds or not high enough to clear the net.

Athletes can practice daily for hours and work on specific muscle-memory techniques, mental game plans, and tactics to improve their abilities. However, come game day, they can still lose. Professional baseball players can practice hitting pitches hundreds of times at various speeds and curves. When game day arrives, and they are up at the plate, they might strike out several times. Failure occurs because not all variables can be accounted for or worked into practice.

Suppose you put hours of practice toward a particular exam or months of dedication toward a career move. When faced with the moment to present your skills, there is still a chance to fail. Practice does not guarantee success. You can still fail when you think you have studied enough because you did well on the practice problems and homework assignments. Additionally, falling short can occur at work when you feel you did enough to make good marks on your yearly performance appraisal. In all life's cases, unforeseen variables are the most difficult to anticipate. Failure can even occur when driving from point A to point B, even for a cautious driver.

How can a person reduce the likelihood of failure? From my experience, the key is to practice until the chance of failure ceases to exist. Instead of practicing only until you get something right, aim to practice until the potential for failure fades. For instance, when preparing for an academic exam, work on homework problems not until you solve one correctly, but until several are not wrong. Another example is to keep revising your public speaking notes until you can explain them without continually referring to them. It's this practice that turns possible disappointments into success moments.

Continuous dedication to practice is essential for turning potential failures into successes. When swinging a bat to hit a ball, work at it for a while. Do not stop after accomplishing your first couple of hits. This is only the beginning of your efforts. Keep practicing your technique with better swing form and body mechanics until missing becomes rare. Continue pushing yourself to hit the ball as often as possible, and you will see evidence of failure fading.

As you work towards your 'go until you cannot miss,' remember there's always more to learn. Embrace humility and acknowledge that you don't know as much as you think you do. This mindset will keep you open-minded and receptive to new learning. Furthermore, whatever you're working towards, keep at it. The time and effort you invest will eventually become second nature and an instinctive part of your daily routine. Continuous improvement is the path to reaching a threshold where failure is no longer an option.

It is common knowledge that new undertakings will have their share of unknown variables and challenges. Therefore, it is common for people to fail a few times on the way to their first triumph or first success. Riding a bicycle is a good example. A beginning bicyclist may lean heavily to one side and even fall off entirely. However, with dedication and a willingness to keep trying, a beginning rider becomes more stable and stops falling off. They have reached a threshold in their ability where it would take a lot to knock them off. Being open to learning and welcoming challenges paves the way for success. As a result, you'll find that success happens more often than failure.

Using the novice cyclist analogy, the key takeaway is to practice consistently until failure becomes infrequent and almost nonexistent. Working toward any new accomplishment involves a balancing act of failures and successes. When outcomes lead to infrequent failures, the notion of success goes beyond having succeeded once or twice. The success rate is well below the failure rate by a wide margin. Therefore, the focus of this entire process is not just on understanding how something can be achieved, but on comprehending how it must be carried out to avoid failure.

Reaching the point of infrequent failure signifies a high level of mastery, where failing becomes more challenging than producing a correct result. While working toward your accomplishments, you become so proficient at what you do that getting it right becomes easier than failing. In other words, you have reached a level of competence and ability where failure is no longer common but an exception. Hence, the chapter title, 'Keep Going Until Failure Fades.'

Returning to an earlier example regarding education, when preparing for exams, many students practice until they understand the material and can answer problems correctly. However, this approach may not be sufficient, especially for specific subjects like math. For instance, students might work on problems until they feel confident in their answers, but this may not guarantee success.

In humanities courses such as history, literature, and communications, students can reread sections of chapters and review class notes until they are familiar with the concepts. Then, they can write down their thoughts and ideas during a test by paraphrasing their notes. Passing these courses has little to do with perfection and more with gaining an overall understanding. Thus, failure can be avoided by following reasonable practices. However, this may not be enough for success on math-based exams that require specific calculations and precise answers instead of generalities.

Becoming familiar with the material is not the same as genuinely mastering it. Mastery involves applying your knowledge in various situations, explaining concepts to others, and tackling complex problems. Math-based tests have right and wrong answers, unlike many humanities courses, where answers can be subjective. Therefore, to achieve specific results (e.g., calculation), you should focus on minimizing the risk of failure by practicing until mistakes are nearly eliminated. When failure fades during practice, the likelihood of encountering unexpected information during an exam is significantly reduced.

To succeed in practice, it's crucial to reduce the likelihood of failure and showcase your skills effectively.

This emphasizes the pivotal role of consistent practice. Picture a situation where the exam duration is reduced by 10 to 15 minutes, yet completion remains necessary. Prior practice focused on success will account for adverse conditions such as this. Additionally, imagine a testing environment that may not be ideal yet still demands the completion of the exam. You can confidently overcome these challenges through maximized practice, focusing on minimizing failure.

Practicing a process where failing ceases to exist means shifting your perspective on failure. Instead of seeing failure as a negative outcome, view it as a learning opportunity. Challenging yourself by working through tasks slightly beyond your current abilities. Once you have a firm handle on what you are trying to accomplish and have practiced it to a point where you feel confident about your physical, educational, or occupational abilities, create obstacles for yourself that put your abilities under pressure to perform the same successful results.

If you're working toward being more competitive in sports, one thing you could do is practice in adverse weather conditions. Professional athletes use this process to challenge themselves to work harder and stay focused. They feed themselves with pressure in practice to perform better, faster, and more efficiently in games. A basketball player will take on two players at practice to make game situations seem more effortless. Chess players will challenge several opponents at once. Being pressured is a tactic used to increase one's skills and ability.

A quarterback standing in one place and completing passes to receivers is relatively easy. But a quarterback being chased by defensive linemen while trying to make the same pass will be challenging. A tennis player striking a tennis ball well when standing at the center of the baseline is not too difficult. However, chasing down a tennis ball on the run is difficult when the ball is moving away from you at an angle. Therefore, the challenge is to strike the ball so it arcs back over the net with pace and accuracy when out of a comfort zone.

If you want to be successful at whatever you do, you must practice doing things well and put obstacles in your path to simulate variables that may occur while testing your achievements. Overcoming obstacles during practice, from academics to athletics, will make the test on those skills appear much more manageable. Not being so comfortable in practice and forcing yourself to overcome failure will make the testing more comfortable. Hence, the chapter's title is 'Keep Going Until Failure Fades.'

Perhaps your situation does not involve academics or athletics, but instead a presentation. If this is the case, how about practicing the presentation with missing PowerPoint slides so that when you give the actual presentation, you feel confident you can fill in the missing information if your materials let you down? If the presentation is not a PowerPoint but deals with computations, give yourself less time in practice so you will not feel pressured if you are given less time during your presentation. Moreover, once you fully grasp the material, try practicing your skills in situations that annoy you, such as noise and other distractions. See how you can handle distractions in your presentation so you can get through them if any occur during your actual presentation.

If you want to improve at what you do and get past the point of repetitive failures, you need to be challenged by yourself and others; nobody becomes excellent at what they do without it. Being challenged by others is essential for improving your ability to navigate and learn from potential failures. When others challenge you, they reveal areas where your knowledge or skills may be lacking—academically, physically, emotionally, or behaviorally. Being challenged by others exposes you to new perspectives, pushing you to exceed your limits and to think outside the box.

Being challenged by others can be uncomfortable and intimidating, yet it is essential for personal growth and development. Embrace competition with those more skilled than you, as this allows you to learn and improve. As you gain experience, you become a stronger competitor. With increased competence, you will encounter fewer failures; as you fail less, you find greater enjoyment in your pursuits. This enjoyment fuels your motivation. Ultimately, the more you enjoy what you do, the fewer failures you will face.

Remember, practicing anything until you get it right is only the beginning of success. There is a long road ahead if you wish to push practice until failure fades. Don't give up; many people have pushed past this initial point and gone on to have successful journeys. These people have learned from others or gained experience in what it takes to succeed. They may even have felt motivated by their accomplishments, driven to compete with others who have acquired the same or similar abilities in a comparable field.

Embarking on a new journey can be likened to joining a study group, where the collaborative effort transforms your understanding and elevates your grades from consistent Cs to a B average. Taking on this challenge to mix with strong students will support the drive to practice until failure fades. Similarly, participating in sports alongside more skilled athletes can elevate your abilities, transforming you from a novice just learning the basics to a semi-pro who confidently navigates complexities and showcases improved skills. Taking on this challenge to mix with strong athletes will support the drive to practice until failure fades.

Continually challenging yourselves and pushing your limits, you are on your way to being good at what you do. However, simply starting down a path isn't enough to avoid failure. It takes more than mixing with the right talents to achieve successful outcomes. To be the best, you must keep moving beyond where most people are comfortable stopping. You must go beyond the average that most people are satisfied with. You must reach out along different avenues to learn various skills and bring that understanding into your world. You must challenge yourself progressively and allow yourself to be challenged by others with stronger talents and abilities. This determination and focus, along with the challenges posed by others, will reduce the likelihood of failure when tested against yourself or others.

Keep working toward your goal with intention and purposeful practices. Remember, practice not until you succeed but until failure becomes nonexistent. By intentionally practicing, you will build your knowledge base, physical skills, and abilities, setting yourself apart from others who have rested on their prior accomplishments. Those willing to challenge themselves and be challenged by others reach a higher threshold where failing ceases to exist. I encourage you to follow in the footsteps of those exceptional individuals who stand out in academics, careers, athletics, music, or any field where you aspire to leave your mark.

Do not stop progressing because you have reached a level beyond those around you. Keep pushing yourself past the point you thought was not possible for anyone. Keep in mind that it is okay to fail when going beyond those around you; it happens a lot to those who push themselves to be great at what they do. Beyond the failures is a new and better you—a person forged by hard work and discipline. Let hard work become part of your routine. Realize that the same hard work and discipline must have been accomplished by others you have passed and those you have yet to reach, waiting at the top.

Hard work and discipline are readily evident in the Big 3: education, sports, and music. Our society is comprised of successful people who have worked hard to build their education and knowledge and now own successful companies. The sports world comprises successful and talented athletes who break records, make it look easy, and inspire others. The music industry is also full of successful and talented musicians who have challenged themselves to be the best. Beautiful singers and gifted writers who are excellent at what they do make it look easy and inspire others through constant practice, which has led their failures to fade.

If you aspire to succeed, you must work for it. Don't stop learning about your craft or trying to understand it better. This is only the beginning of the journey. Keep going until failure in your actions becomes a thing of the past. Seek out those who have already succeeded and reached the top. This could mean networking with successful individuals in your desired field, reading biographies of accomplished people, or attending seminars and workshops to expand your knowledge and skills. When you stumble, don't let it deter you. Remember, challenges are inevitable in the pursuit of success. Continually overcoming failures will propel you to the top, where failures are virtually nonexistent.

Chapter 16
Incorporate the Linear not Curvilinear

Things do not always go as planned. We have to make room for imperfection in our lives. Those imperfect moments are the moments we grow the most.

— **Cara Alwill Leyba**

If we know exactly where we're going, exactly how to get there, and exactly what we'll see along the way, we won't learn anything.

— **M. Scott Peck**

Life is a tapestry of events, each following different trajectories—linear, curvilinear, or exponential. Linear events, in particular, provide a sense of control and comfort because they can be planned for. You can anticipate these events, adjust your schedule, and prepare for a second attempt if you miss the first one. This predictability can be empowering, giving you more control over your life's direction. When the outcomes of events are clear and straightforward, they belong to the linear category. Making sensible decisions in linear situations can significantly decrease life's unpredictability, leading to a stable life.

Other examples of linear events include scheduled academic exams, planned vacations, and routine doctor's appointments. A planned family dinner is linear, while a sudden car breakdown is curvilinear due to the variables involved in the breakdown and repair. Another example of a linear event could be a regular exercise routine. In contrast, a curvilinear event could be a sudden injury that disrupts the routine and hampers several other areas of your life. Surprise parties and unexpected work tasks are complex because they involve many more variables than straightforward planning. Curvilinear (unpredictable) events could be a sudden illness, a natural disaster, or a surprise marriage proposal.

Life is filled with unpredictable events, which I consider curvilinear. Planning for these events and anticipating their outcome can be a significant challenge, if not impossible. These unexpected events do not fit into a straight line where you can estimate or calculate what will happen before or after them. It is like being pitched a curveball. They are curvilinear because the unknown arc is difficult to read and respond to, adding complexity and unpredictability to the event. However, in these moments of unpredictability, our adaptability is tested, making us more resilient and capable.

Unlike curvilinear and exponential events (things that start slowly but quickly get out of hand), linear events have a few highly predictable outcomes, making them easier to manage. For example, consider buying a lottery ticket. If you hold onto the ticket, you will encounter just three scenarios: you can win, lose, or earn a free ticket. These are linear events where you have some control. If you win, you can keep the money or buy another ticket. If you lose, you can walk away or purchase another ticket. If you win a free ticket, you will face these three possibilities again.

Comparing linear outcomes to life reveals that linear events are more straightforward than those affected by unpredictability. External forces have a minimal impact on linear events. In daily life, you can anticipate what to expect and even make accurate short-term predictions by planning for certain events to occur or not occur. Similarly, straight lines are predictable and follow a one-to-one relationship; when one event occurs, another, as anticipated, usually follows. Straight lines do not have unexpected bends. This makes dealing with linear events more manageable.

However, curvilinear experiences do have turns and bends (unpredictable) and are not one-to-one, meaning there is no understandable action and reaction. When one event happens or unfolds, there is a good chance that the outcome will not be anticipated. It may happen the way you expected, but it may not. Consequently, planning for the unexpected is much more challenging than preparing for the intended and predictable. Therefore, linear events are easier to handle than curvilinear ones, so it's advisable to focus on incorporating linear experiences into your life rather than curvilinear ones.

Life events often exhibit high short-term predictability, particularly over a day or a week. For instance, daily routines such as commuting to work or attending classes at school typically follow a well-established schedule, creating a familiar rhythm in our lives during these brief periods. If you reflect on your routine from the past few days, you'll likely find that your activities mirror those you anticipate in the upcoming days. You may follow a consistent route to your workplace or school, frequently passing by the same cafés, shops, or parks. Furthermore, your interactions will often be with the same individuals—colleagues, classmates, or friends—strengthening the sense of familiarity and predictability. This cyclical nature of daily life offers a comforting stability, allowing us to plan, anticipate, and manage our time effectively.

This predictability can be comforting because it provides a sense of security. However, a linear approach can become unpredictable based on the friends you keep and their suggestions for your life. This adds a layer of uncertainty. As a result, because of others' input, there is an element of unpredictability, and it is impossible to accurately predict the outcomes of events in your life one, five, or even ten years down the line. Because of this, it is important to have friends who also live somewhat predictable lives, with little risk and no defiance of the law.

A curvilinear lifestyle can quickly get out of hand when dealing with unknown variables. Associating with like-minded individuals can help keep you grounded and your life in order, preventing unpredictable events from overwhelming you. Since adverse events occur randomly, it is important to maintain a close relationship with linear events (as predictable as possible).

The 2007 financial crisis was unexpected. It was also likely unpredictable in its early stages of growth, leading to economic world chaos. It came on suddenly and unfolded quickly. Many companies worldwide went bankrupt. Property values plummeted, millions could not pay their mortgages, and millions more were at risk of losing their homes. The days leading up to the event were linear, but if someone had planned their life from 2005 through 2007, they would never have been able to prepare for it. This is because events in the world, led by others, play havoc on a linear lifestyle.

The pandemic that began in 2019 served as a stark example of unpredictability. It emerged suddenly and devastated the entire world. The airborne illness hospitalized millions of people, overwhelming hospitals to the point of crisis. Additionally, millions more suffered from the virus's effects without being able to reach a hospital. According to the United Nations Department of Economic and Social Affairs (2024), an estimated 7 million deaths are attributed to the COVID-19 pandemic.

The entire world came to a halt. Who could have foreseen that millions would lose their lives to a severe airborne virus or that nearly every business would face significant financial challenges as a result? More than a year elapsed before a reliable vaccine was developed, and it took almost two years for many businesses to regain their financial footing, with some enduring a much longer recovery. If this isn't unpredictability at its finest, I don't know what is.

When considering time, such as weeks, months, and years, most life is not linear but curvilinear (unpredictable). However, on any given day, we think life is predictable (linear) because we are creatures of habit, and our daily routines and schedules are familiar to us. In a way, these habits create a sense of predictability. But most living life is curvilinear and unpredictable. In a nutshell, unpredictable events lead to even more unpredictable events, and the chain reaction becomes increasingly erratic.

Think of it in this manner: if unforeseen events keep happening, it will remain a new situation. In this regard, we are always on 'new ground,' which means we constantly face new and unpredictable situations. The 'new ground' idea emphasizes the need for adaptability in decision-making. It reminds us to be prepared for the unexpected. If we can highlight the importance of adaptability, we will feel less anxious in the face of uncertainty. Therefore, the best one can hope for is to create a linear experience from unpredictable ones.

Imagine standing on a line. The line stretches out in front of you as far as you can see. If you start steadily walking towards a distant point on this line, you will reach that predetermined point at a specific time. You can also calculate when you will arrive based on your walking speed. Linear events in life follow this metaphor; thus, achieving attainable goals can yield predictable results. For example, attending school fits this model: you enroll in a certain number of courses each term, and after completing several terms, you will achieve your educational goals.

It is important to strive for predictability, especially amid unpredictable and chaotic events. Predictability allows you to plan, adjust, and maintain consistency. When you discover a process that works for you and helps you progress, stick with it. Fight for predictability by creating consistency in your daily activities. Using the example above of taking courses, when things become difficult, and you might fail a course (causing unpredictability in your graduation, finances, etc.), fight to regain a linear lifestyle by getting more help to pass the course.

It's important to remember that unpredictability is part of life, and it's only a matter of time before it tries to throw you off your path. The key to dealing with it is adaptability. When unpredictability throws you off your path, be ready to adapt and make the necessary adjustments. This reassurance that adaptability is the key will help you navigate the unpredictability that life throws your way with confidence. Keep aiming for the predictable so that life remains manageable.

While remaining on the subject, it's important to acknowledge that chance and timing can disrupt the predictability of events. Once again, life's randomness can be overwhelming. We make hundreds, if not thousands, of conscious decisions each day, and each decision can lead to various unpredictable outcomes. Understanding that there are limits to what can be predicted is crucial.

We cannot manage everything we deal with perfectly or push out all unpredictable events. Accepting this reality is perfectly reasonable; therefore, doing your best is all you can hope to do. It may be possible to predict and manage the outcome of relatively short-term events that you have complete control over; however, it isn't feasible to guarantee a positive outcome every time.

In my fifty-plus years of living, there are two things I know for sure: first, the unpredictable is predictable, and second, opposite outcomes often occur. For instance, when something does not happen as expected, that's an example of the unexpected being predictable. Additionally, when something you initially like or dislike turns out to be different from what was initially anticipated, that's an example of the opposite happening.

You can find this in many places in your life. When you pay attention to events in your life, you'll notice specific patterns. For example, when unprepared, you often find yourself facing troubling circumstances. However, when you are prepared, there is rarely an incident that rises to the level of a worrisome circumstance.

Additionally, when you expect something to be challenging, it turns out to be easier than anticipated. However, when you expect something to be quick and straightforward, it can turn into a tedious task that takes longer than expected. These are examples of opposites. As you can see, even the best-laid plans can change significantly due to unforeseen variances. Therefore, you will have better odds of avoiding the unpredictable and the opposite from occurring if you can make your life more predictable through sound decision-making.

Sound decision-making will lead to more predictable outcomes than not. This is because good decisions often lead to predictable outcomes and are formed through reasoning and logic. For example, driving home and obeying the speed limit is sensible and will lead to a predictable outcome, such as arriving home safely. The high probability of predictability also leads to other positive outcomes. Let's consider the circumstances of driving home for those who are awaiting your arrival.

Driving while texting is a poor decision and can be dangerous. Such a choice is not based on sound reasoning or logic, as it puts you in a distracted situation. While you might feel comfortable texting and driving occasionally, it can lead to unpredictable and harmful outcomes, such as being pulled over by law enforcement, colliding with another vehicle, hitting an object, or even causing a more serious accident.

Choosing not to text while driving is the best decision, increasing the likelihood of a safe and predictable outcome. Choosing not to text and drive means you can arrive at your destination without incident. With this example, predictability is important because it helps ensure the safety of both you and others on the road. Hence, predictable events often lead to more predictable events. What can also be deduced from this example is that unpredictable events often lead to more unexpected events.

According to the National Highway Traffic Safety Administration (NHTSA), 3,308 people died in car crashes caused by distracted drivers in 2022. As a driver, it is crucial to anticipate other drivers' actions, which may require your full attention to avoid a collision. However, if you are distracted by texting, you won't be able to maintain that necessary focus, increasing the risk of an incident. The potential outcomes of texting and driving can be severe, including personal injury and legal repercussions. This highlights the importance of making good decisions.

When we examine driving while texting more closely, we see that distracted driving can quickly and easily lead to disruptive events that significantly affect people's lives. As a young adult, minimizing the likelihood of unforeseen situations is important; events like these often escalate into riskier behavior. Furthermore, these events may become more erratic, which is usually unavoidable. Therefore, avoiding situations that could lead to unexpected outcomes is crucial. Since mistakes tend to compound over time, the fewer unpredictable experiences you encounter in your youth, the more stable you will be as an adult.

Linear events from good choices often generate simple questions and straightforward answers. Responses to linear events are usually yes, no, and other direct replies. In contrast, curvilinear events from poor choices have a significant personal impact and generate many difficult questions. Here are some potential questions that could arise from driving while texting and resulting in a collision. How badly are you injured? How severe are the injuries to others? Was anyone in your vehicle or theirs injured, and to what extent? How badly damaged are the vehicles? How much will your insurance rates increase? Are you at risk of losing your license or having it suspended?

These questions are not just hypothetical; they are reasonable questions about the consequences of a single poor decision. In retrospect, making good choices consistently for a better life is essential. One bad choice can lead to others, creating a chain reaction. As a result, the outcomes of compounded poor decisions can become highly unpredictable. A simple event, such as driving while distracted, shows how quickly life can shift from predictable (arriving safely at your destination) to unpredictable (being liable for damages and potentially injuring others).

Reasonable and logical decisions should be made to reduce life's unpredictability. The previous example was texting and driving, but there are hundreds of similar life-altering events you should make predictable in your life. Living a healthy life by avoiding drugs and excessive drinking makes life predictable, so don't start making life unpredictable. Living around people who make good decisions not to cheat, steal, or harm others makes life predictable; thus, don't start making it unpredictable.

It may sound boring to make good decisions repeatedly, but it is much better than suffering the consequences of unforeseen events when things turn sour. Making sound decisions involves avoiding adverse outcomes; it fosters a stable, secure life filled with positive, predictable outcomes. Sound decisions based on reflection and foresight do not lead you into unstable situations, such as legal trouble.

Good or bad, right or wrong, events build on other events. By attempting to make all your life events as linear (predictable, purposeful, calculated) as possible, you gain control over the outcomes in your life.

Life is already unpredictable, so why add more to it? You have the power to make sound, sensible decisions; don't let anyone tell you otherwise. Remember, you have the freedom to choose, but not the freedom to escape the consequences of your choices. Good decisions generally lead to stable and predictable outcomes, allowing you to build a solid foundation for your future. When you make thoughtful choices, you take control of your direction and create a life that is easier to navigate.

Using a simple analogy: sound decisions are like straight lines—predictable, with future points that can be estimated. Poor decisions, on the other hand, resemble curved lines—their twists are more complicated to anticipate, making the path ahead uncertain and unstable.

Critical Thinking and Pride

Pride is commonly understood as the satisfaction or pleasure individuals feel from their accomplishments, reflecting a positive acknowledgment of their abilities and efforts. This emotion can manifest as a sense of healthy self-esteem, recognizing one's worth and capabilities while maintaining a balanced perspective. Pride can inspire motivation, encourage personal growth, and foster resilience in the face of challenges.

However, when pride becomes excessive, it can tip into arrogance, characterized by an overinflated sense of self-importance and entitlement. This shift not only skews one's self-awareness but can also lead to negative interpersonal dynamics, as arrogance often alienates others and hinders meaningful connections. Ultimately, while a moderate amount of pride can enhance well-being and confidence, it is important to remain vigilant against its more detrimental forms, ensuring that self-esteem is grounded in reality rather than inflated by an egoistic perspective.

Grasping the complex negative emotions stemming from excessive pride is vital for personal growth and self-awareness. While often viewed as a positive trait, pride can sometimes cross the line into conceit. This undesirable quality alienates others and can erode one's self-esteem over time. This undermining effect can manifest in feelings of inadequacy or isolation despite an outward appearance of confidence. It's important to be aware of the destructive consequences of unchecked pride; recognizing these pitfalls can foster healthier relationships and a more balanced self-view.

As one can see, pride is a complex term referring to positive and negative traits. On the one hand, it may represent proper behavior or virtues such as self-esteem, self-acceptance, and self-confidence; on the other, it can signify corruption and arrogance. Understanding pride requires careful consideration of how it is expressed. Therefore, managing pride effectively involves awareness and critical thinking skills. By using these tools, we can explore their negative aspects, such as arrogance and mental corruption, as well as their positive facets. This process fosters introspection and mindfulness, helping us understand how pride influences our lives, both positively and negatively.

In a work environment, pride is a powerful tool for boosting self-confidence and building self-esteem. These two qualities are essential as they form the foundation for developing distinct aspects of strong, lasting character. Self-confidence refers to the belief in one's abilities, while self-esteem reflects the value one places on one's skills and accomplishments. Critical thinking is key to managing pride and preventing self-confidence and self-esteem from inflating into arrogance. This being said, a critical thinker understands that success depends on many variables, such as timing and luck.

A person must take pride in their work, but they should also be able to differentiate between self-confidence and arrogance. Excessive pride can lead to overconfidence, which can come across as conceit. This distinction highlights the fine line between self-confidence and arrogance, where critical thinking is vital to staying mindful and avoiding crossing that line. Self-confidence and the grounding effect of humility reassure individuals and help them stay on the humble side of this boundary.

Developing critical thinking skills related to a person's actions and how others may perceive them is crucial for understanding self-confidence and self-esteem. These awareness skills help us evaluate the boundaries of our behavior, fostering a healthy environment for self-confidence and self-esteem. However, it's important to remember that we risk losing our humility when pride dominates our thoughts, emotions, and actions. Therefore, it is good to know that balancing confidence with self-esteem can foster personal growth and inspire those who witness our progress.

What is your definition of *pride*? Write clearly and concisely here:

How is *pride* tied to critical thinking?

How has your *pride* (or lack of) impacted your life up to this point?

How do critical thinking skills strengthen a person's sense of *pride*?

Explain how developing a progressive sense of *pride* can positively impact a person's life.

Explain how the absence of developing a sense of *pride* may hurt a person's life. (For instance, avoiding potential dangers, understanding personal emotions, etc.)

Express how you feel about *pride* being one of the most essential things in a successful life. (You may need to define the term successful.)

Chapter 17
Take It to a Higher Power

A body of men holding themselves accountable to nobody ought not to be trusted by anybody.

— **Thomas Paine**

A person may cause evil to others not only by his actions but by his inaction, and in either case he is justly accountable to them for the injury.

— **John Stuart Mill**

Every individual possesses inherent limitations that influence their ability to comprehend complex concepts, process logical information, and engage in practical reasoning. While some concepts and logic are easily grasped due to their straightforward nature, others remain elusive and challenging. These cognitive limitations that a person encounters can stem from various sources, including innate predispositions—meaning some individuals may be naturally inclined toward certain types of understanding—or environmental factors, such as educational exposure and life experiences, that shape cognitive development.

As a result, our mental capacities serve as a framework that can either expand or restrict our ability to fully grasp and engage with ideas communicated by others. This dynamic means that each person has unique thresholds for receiving, interpreting, and processing information. Such distinctions highlight the importance of personalized approaches that do not rely on one-size-fits-all.

Moreover, just as cognitive abilities vary, so too do physical capabilities. Everyone showcases a distinct range of physical skills and abilities influenced by genetics, training, and personal experience. This combination of influences further illustrates the complexity of each person's potential to engage with what they do, whether physical, emotional, or psychological. As a result, the world showcases a wide variety of human experiences and abilities. People could significantly improve their interactions and environments if they recognized and embraced these intellectual and physical capacities.

For example, some people have physical abilities such as running fast and jumping high, while others may struggle. Individuals also exhibit various personality traits; some deflect negativity, while others absorb it. The unique combination of these traits contributes to their diversity. Thus, physical abilities and emotional and cognitive characteristics set people apart.

In contrast, because our underlying emotional structures and human qualities are similar, shared experiences often trigger common feelings such as happiness, sadness, and disappointment. What makes one person generally happy can be the same for another. Moreover, what makes one person sad or disappointed can be the same for another. This being said, there are limits and boundaries to how far individuals can be separated from one another in these areas of influence (physical, psychological, emotional, etc.).

Although it is up to each person to determine how they respond to these physical and emotional events, there is a limit to what we can physically and mentally achieve when shaping our lives and creating the world we desire. Therefore, it is essential to prioritize self-preservation and how we process and engage with the information around us. It's important to recognize that we must care for ourselves before we can effectively help others. This should not be viewed as selfishness; instead, it's about maintaining balance in our lives and positioning ourselves to assist others. This perspective helps us understand that self-care is a foundational step toward supporting those around us.

Placing yourself in a favorable environment fosters a mindset where your needs are prioritized. However, it's important to also look beyond your personal needs to help others when appropriate; this embodies the essence of caring for those around you. This approach is often seen as living under a higher power, higher principles, or a system of values in which others are viewed as just as necessary. Think of a higher power as a set of guiding principles or belief systems that significantly influence the moral compass. It acts like a compass, always pointing us in the right direction and offering reassurance and guidance in our actions.

Believing in the fundamental importance of honesty shapes the way you communicate and interact with others. It prompts you to consistently convey the truth, even when doing so may be challenging or uncomfortable. This unwavering commitment to honesty cultivates trust in your relationships, establishing a foundation for open and genuine interactions.

Similarly, a dedication to acting with compassion drives you to offer assistance to those in need, even when such actions may require personal sacrifice or discomfort. This commitment often prompts you to step outside your comfort zone, whether by volunteering your time, listening to someone in distress, or trying to alleviate others' burdens, regardless of the inconvenience it may bring to your own life.

These guiding principles serve as a framework for maintaining essential personal attributes such as compassion, integrity, and honesty. They act as a moral compass, steering your decisions and actions towards what is ethically correct and empathetic, helping you navigate the complexities of life with clarity and purpose. In this way, your values become a steadfast guide, ensuring you remain aligned with your deeper principles, no matter your circumstances.

Merely believing you are 'good' is not enough, as the concept of 'good' is universally ambiguous. Creating limits and boundaries of 'good' and 'acceptable' holds little weight. For example, retaliating against another's actions may seem acceptable (just), but it may not necessarily be reasonable. Modifying rules to satisfy personal preferences may appear reasonable (good) in certain situations, but it is ultimately neither right nor fair to others. This perspective, and those like it, emphasize the importance of personal responsibility and accountability to a higher standard.

Personal responsibility is a powerful tool that enables us to recognize the impact of our actions on others and to ensure they align with moral and ethical values. It requires us to stay in tune with our conscience, which guides our decisions and actions. Being accountable to a higher standard provides checks and balances of critical thinking, preventing us from rationalizing intentional errors as mere coincidences, blaming others, or dismissing wrongdoing with excuses like, 'That's just how it worked out.'

Ultimately, responsibility and ownership of one's actions are the keys to shaping our lives and world. This chapter is not about promoting a specific religion but about understanding the role of a 'higher power' in our lives. The term' higher power' is used here to represent a guiding force that helps individuals make ethical decisions and act morally responsibly. When I refer to a 'higher power,' I am not necessarily speaking of a specific deity or religious figure. Rather, I mean a source of authority beyond yourself—something to which you hold yourself accountable, that guides your behavior, and that you turn to for emotional and spiritual support. If you choose, this chapter can be understood through that lens.

Instead, I'm referring to a moral and ethical framework, a set of principles, or a belief system that guides our actions. This 'high power' situated outside our desires guides us in doing right, whether it benefits us or not, and steers us away from doing wrong, even if we could get away with it. This sense of a 'higher power' is the internal obligation to act honorably and be committed to fair practices at all times with everyone.

Since everyone has the freedom to choose and act on right and wrong, a 'higher power' is meant to be a sounding board for cognitive and spiritual reflection. When discussing a higher power, I have identified three viewpoints: those who are spiritually committed to a higher power, those who acknowledge a higher power when it suits their needs, and those who do not believe in any higher power.

In my experience, people who do not believe in a higher power may find it challenging to stay connected to their moral compass when caring for others, especially when they encounter their own limitations. I've also observed they may struggle with critical thinking skills, which can impede their ability to safeguard themselves and others from psychological and emotional harm. These situations typically arise from the priorities individuals set for themselves and the degree of responsibility they choose to assume. I will provide an example of this later.

Not believing in a higher power resonates with individuals who consider themselves their own authority and often position themselves at the center of situations to take advantage of irregularities. For them, life is what they choose to make of it, and 'just by chance,' the pendulum most always swings in their favor; how convenient. This happens because these individuals become their own guiding force in the absence of a higher power. They craft their rules as they navigate life, convincing themselves their actions are justified.

Some may argue that believing in a higher power is unnecessary for personal accountability and moral guidance. However, from my experiences and observations, I know otherwise. Without a higher power, individuals on the fence with moral decisions struggle to maintain a strong moral compass, harming themselves and others. The harm to themselves and others is significant when they do not adhere to a higher power's guidance. It can lead to a lack of personal integrity, a strained relationship, and moral confusion.

These consequences, lack of personal integrity, hurtful relationships, and moral confusion, are not to be underestimated since they pose an adverse risk to strengthening friendships. Therefore, each area should be considered carefully in any decision-making process. However, the outcome can be severely skewed if the process focuses solely on how a person feels about their conscience while acting as their own authority (a higher power). Consequently, taking shortcuts at strategic moments in life and making up rules as one goes along to justify actions is not the best way to live. And it is undoubtedly not the process of living under a high power.

A higher power provides a moral and ethical framework for making difficult decisions. A framework positioned outside oneself provides a set of principles and a system that guide one's actions, with stronger principles than one has for oneself. Without such a guiding force (outside oneself), a person's mind and heart lack an external force to hold them accountable.

They become their own guides and do whatever they think is in their best interest, regardless of how it may affect others. Thus, nothing is in a position to question this person's motives or agenda. They are left to their own conscience on whatever feels right to them in whatever circumstance they find themselves in. They are holding themselves accountable, like a fox in charge of the hen house.

When people hold themselves accountable, they can change the rules to match what they consider right and wrong. They are not obligated to follow social rules, etiquette, or human decency since their outcomes will be whatever they want. However, this freedom does not absolve them of the consequences of their actions.

Suppose the person holding themselves accountable for their actions does something wrong or harmful to others, according to any human society's standards. In that case, that person justifies it by changing the rules and making an exception for the occurrence. To them, there is no accountability, remorse, or reconciliation for breaking the laws of man or God.

As Albert Einstein posits, problems cannot be solved at the same level of thinking in which they were created. Knowing this, we see that life often presents us with situations where actions are complex, and people may be tempted to skirt obligations and human decency to gain an advantage. Fixing adverse events becomes hard—sometimes impossible—when the person deciding what can be changed is emotionally tied to the outcome. In these moments, the absence of a higher power guiding their conscience leads to a skewed view of ethical living, where they feel justified in their actions when the time calls for it.

Their views of ethical living are skewed in their favor when they feel the time is favorable for them. Therefore, it's crucial to remember that ethical living is not a matter of convenience but a fundamental aspect of our character and integrity. In the context of a higher power, ethical living means living by the principles and values set by that higher power, which often include love, compassion, and integrity. On this note, let me share a story with you.

I have a good friend; we have been friends for about 28 years. We both believe in Christ and have always had a platonic Christian friendship. Since she lives quite a distance away, I only get to visit her once a year, maybe even less often. When we meet, we talk about life, hike on trails, and share time with her parents and friends. This is a time I have always enjoyed and will have fond memories of.

A few years back, I went to visit her during the summer, and we spent some time hiking together. She confided in me that she had met someone and was considering starting a relationship with him. I inquired if the person shared our faith and values. She said he is not a believer (to me, this means he has no higher power). I gently cautioned her that it might be a rocky relationship because, from my experience, those who do not position themselves under the authority of a higher power tend to make up the rules as they go through life. They justify their actions as they see fit. Individuals who are not held accountable to anyone but themselves can interpret right and wrong based on their personal beliefs.

These personal beliefs can run counter to human decency and integrity.

Months later, I checked in with her over the phone to see how things were progressing. She said things were good, and the relationship was moving up the ladder of intimacy. By 'ladder of intimacy,' I mean the relationship progressed from casual to more serious and committed. Again, I briefly shared my thoughts with her and left it at that. We are both adults, and I cannot decide for her or force my views on her.

A few more months passed, and I had the opportunity to visit the following summer. I drove the long distance to her place and spent the weekend catching up while hiking. The conversation about relationships arose, and I asked how things were going. She said the person she was seeing was no longer in the picture. This prompted my question: How did this come to be? Then she told me.

One day, she visited his house to bring him soup to help him feel better since he had been unwell the previous week. After knocking on the door, a girl answered and introduced herself. During a brief conversation, it became clear that this girl was his long-term girlfriend of four years. My friend mentioned that she had been in a physical and committed relationship with him for over a year. Meanwhile, my friend had no idea she was the 'other woman,' the one the guy was seeing behind his girlfriend's back. Both girls were incredibly upset about the situation. My friend walked away from the house and the relationship a lot wiser.

After hearing this story, I expressed my sympathy for what had happened. As we continued the hike, my thoughts reaffirmed the importance of accountability. Without the concept of an externally positioned higher power resonating in a person's heart and mind, that person holds themselves accountable for their actions; they can justify their means however they want. These people can have no rhythm or reason for their actions other than their pleasure and security.

This concept is not about perfection; we all stumble in many ways. But I believe those committed to living a life under a higher power, an authority beyond themselves, will do much less damage to others. This is because the higher power's accountability, honor, and commitment create a model and a consistent framework that does not fluctuate with events or circumstances.

The takeaway: when you become involved with others on a friendship level or deeper, it's important to determine whether they hold themselves accountable for their actions or a higher power to guide them. Those acting in their own authority can adjust their principles of integrity, honesty, and commitment as situations demand, rationalizing their choices to free themselves from accountability. You don't want to be involved with these people. A purposeful, well-structured life is often found among those who genuinely care for one another. Those who care for each other are frequently guided by authority rather than considering themselves their own authority.

Chapter 18
Ninety-nine and One are the Same Result

The first step towards true enlightenment is to lighten up on yourself.

— **Bashar**

How you spend your time is ultimately your decision, reflecting your values and priorities. When you cultivate a consistent routine around activities that resonate with you—whether related to personal growth, hobbies, or work—minor disruptions and setbacks tend to diminish your overall focus and enthusiasm. This steadfast dedication fosters momentum, helping you remain engaged and motivated even when faced with challenges.

Conversely, even slight inconveniences can feel significantly disruptive if you have yet to establish a reliable routine or are still contemplating the importance of consistency in your pursuits. In such cases, the lack of a structured approach can lead to frustration or distraction, making it challenging to stay aligned with your goals. Thus, developing a clear and consistent pattern of engaging in meaningful activities enhances your productivity and equips you with the resilience to navigate life's inevitable interruptions more effectively.

While you have the freedom to spend your time as you wish, not discovering something meaningful will ultimately be your responsibility. Hence, being consistent with your activities and moving toward success is entirely your doing. You are in control of your discipline and motivation. Ultimately, it's all about balancing what truly matters to you. Keep in mind that setbacks and obstacles are a regular part of any journey. Therefore, being upset about the inconveniences that disrupt your routine should be on your shoulders, rather than on external circumstances or others.

If you exercise every day, follow a balanced diet, and consistently maintain good habits, you've likely developed a routine. Suppose you miss a workout day because a friend asks for help, an unexpected errand comes up, or a work project takes up your time. Missing one day of exercise will not undermine all the progress you've made over the past months. Your consistency and dedication have led to significant improvements; one missed day does not erase that effort.

Suppose you had ninety-nine days of working out, and your friend needed your support; it was an emergency. If this is the case, missing one workout will not change much to your overall accomplishments. Ninety-nine times have created a significant difference in your life, and one interruption cannot change it. One missed opportunity does not negate the impact of the ninety-nine times you've succeeded. Therefore, there's no need to be disheartened or frustrated with your friend because of the inconvenience.

Achieving success ninety-nine times is a significant feat and should be a source of pride. View the ninety-nine successful days as significant victories and the one missed day as a natural part of living with other burdens or unforeseen circumstances. The consistency of ninety-nine times places you at the top of any workout chart, and one missed opportunity does not diminish your gains with the ninety-nine. Therefore, succeeding ninety-nine times is fantastic and should be a proud achievement.

Discipline and sacrifice must have been involved in achieving such a long run. You must have sacrificed time in various areas of your life to work out this consistently. You must have made sacrifices elsewhere, since you cannot be in two places at once. Because of this, you should own all the benefits of success that come with working out consistently. However, it's also important to be kind to yourself and understand that life is full of unexpected events. Remember, it's okay to have a disruption. Don't be disappointed in yourself or others for a single missed workout. Instead, focus on the progress you've made and the commitment you've shown, and continue working out consistently.

Let's consider a scenario of inconsistency with a routine. You may have enjoyed exercising once or twice, but it didn't resonate with you, and you didn't continue. Perhaps you started a diet but struggled to maintain it consistently. In this case, 99 days have passed without real effort, discipline, or commitment to a healthy exercise lifestyle. However, things have changed for you. You've developed a new mindset that motivates you to commit to daily workouts and healthier eating. You have successfully completed your first (1) workout in years and are excited for the next one.

Suppose your second day is interrupted: a friend requests help (as in the previous scenario). For whatever reason, you missed the second workout. Missing this second time to work out will not undo any prior progress in past workouts, as this is only the second workout in years. Consistency has not yet been established at this early stage to disrupt significant processes. So, don't be disappointed in yourself or any external events for missing out on the multitude of opportunities to do something when you had the chance and did nothing. You brought the disappointment on yourself.

Remember, it was your choice not to exercise all this time and to put your health in a compromising position. You need to take responsibility for that. If someone requires your help in an emergency or asks you to run an unexpected errand, it's important to recognize that it's not the fault of external events. They shouldn't be blamed for your inconsistencies or for your inability to continue a second time. You chose how to spend your time over the past months. Moreover, a single interruption is unlikely to drastically change your life; your physical appearance will likely remain the same as it was yesterday, when you worked out for the first time. Realize that personal choices shape your outcomes; taking ownership of them is crucial.

Working out once or twice will not change your life meaningfully. Therefore, it would be unfair of you to be disappointed by external factors such as work commitments, family emergencies, or unexpected social events that interrupt your second workout. Consider this: the fact that you've skipped working out ninety-nine times shows that you weren't eager to establish a daily routine to begin with. It was not something you desperately wanted for yourself then, so you should not be too hard on the external events that arise when you begin to show interest again.

In the scenario outlined, you might feel at the lower end of the spectrum compared to others who readily embrace new experiences despite facing challenges in achieving success. These feelings often arise when an individual finds pleasure in a particular activity but becomes disheartened by minor setbacks stemming from inconsistent effort and practice. Such frustration is not uncommon. However, maintaining consistency can be quite challenging without a deep-seated desire and commitment.

When looking at the bigger picture, it's important not to dwell on missed opportunities. Don't be discouraged by what could have been or the benefits you might have gained. The difference that the second or third workout would have made is slight compared to your entire life. If you genuinely wanted to stick to a program, you would have made time for it long ago. The person who has completed ninety-nine workouts in a row was motivated to begin with and has made concessions in other areas to complete such a long run. The best approach in such situations is to handle the interruption, start fresh the following day, and continue your workout as often as possible.

Bringing the two concepts together, the ninety-nine successes with one miss and the ninety-nine misses with one success, there is an underlying philosophy. The philosophical concept here is not to be disappointed with the situation, but to be satisfied with the outcome, because you created it in either case. Do not be upset about being pulled away from completing your hundredth workout; conversely, do not be upset if you cannot string together two in a row. Missing once in one hundred will not change your life; in the same respect, going only once and not making it twice will not make a difference. Both situations have inconsequential outcomes. Their philosophies are the same: neither path will change your life. Missing once will not change your life, and going only once will not either.

Allow yourself the miss and be happy with the ninety-nine times you were successful. Continue your consistency and become tolerant of life's disruptions because you have been consistent. Similarly, do not be disappointed with yourself or others that you only accomplished one or two times out of one hundred. Continue your path after the disruption, and know that you will need to make better choices in how you spend your time in the future. In both scenarios, it is important to accept both outcomes: ninety-nine with one miss and one success with ninety-nine missed opportunities.

Now, it's time to relate this concept to life in general. Be consistent with the things that impact your life, and don't be disappointed if you are imperfect with a disrupted routine. Missing once or twice will not make that much of a difference if you have been consistent. Similarly, don't be disappointed if you missed nearly all the opportunities to impact your life. Accomplishing only once or twice out of many opportunities means you were not motivated for that particular aspect to enter your life.

Find something that you are interested in and make the best of it. Stay calm about the subtle disruptions if you have been consistent. Likewise, stay calm about subtle disruptions if you have not been consistent. An example of this concept that resonates with me is eating organically grown foods. Let's say a person eats organic foods their whole life, but then one day has a meal that isn't organic. That one meal will not offset the health benefits of eating organic their entire life. Conversely, another person has no restrictions on their diet and has never eaten sensibly, then one day decides to have an organic, healthy, sensible meal. That one organic meal will not offset the damaging health situation the person has put themself in over the years. In retrospect, neither life will be changed dramatically.

The concept of 'ninety-nine and one' is a common theme in life. People are consistent in some things and not at all in others. Therefore, do not be frustrated when you miss once, even though you have made a great effort to accomplish many. Likewise, don't be disappointed when you only succeed once and let many opportunities slip by. The results of ninety-nine consistencies and one miss show little effect on the overall accomplishment, just as stringing together one or two consistencies and ninety-nine misses.

If you look at the concept through an application of living life, you can see that the underlying theme in both is knowing that either situation will not drastically affect life. The key is to seize the moment you're given. Don't let opportunities slip by. Therefore, you want to be as consistent as possible in what you put your time and effort into. You want to feel as though you have made progress. However, it's important to understand that life is full of natural and typical inconsistencies, such as unexpected events or other people's needs. These can disrupt your routine indiscriminately, and you want to be ready for them.

If you are consistent in your efforts, a disruption will feel like a welcome break. Viewed another way, if or when disruptions interfere with your routine and force you to miss out on staying consistent with your goals, you will feel much better about giving your time to them if you have spent it wisely up to that point. In contrast, you will feel aggravated by the slightest disruption if you have not spent your time wisely or been consistent with your goals up to that point. As mentioned earlier, it is not the fault of external events or variables; it is yours for not being consistent.

Work diligently and consistently toward your goals when you have the time. Focus on your goals when you are expected to and have the time to do so. Do not allow yourself to be distracted by superficial things along the way. Do not procrastinate; do not put things off until later. Being distracted by unmeaningful things and falling into procreation will not support achievement. Following these simple guidelines will build consistency and make you feel better about your progress.

If you have been consistent in your efforts and made progress over time, an interruption to your schedule will not leave you disappointed. You will have done your best with the time available up to that point. However, suppose you have procrastinated on tasks you should have addressed. In that case, you will feel frustrated and disappointed in yourself and others when you finally start being consistent and face even the slightest interruption.

The concept of 'ninety-nine and one' was something I often experienced during my educational years. I would frequently postpone assignments, basking in a few days of freedom. When I finally decided to start an assignment, by chance, someone would invite me to play ball or join their activities, and I would feel frustrated with them for interrupting me when I had no time to spare. Other times, emergencies would arise at the last minute, diverting my attention from completing my assignments. I would feel upset and overwhelmed by these unexpected situations.

Looking back, I realize these issues were not caused by external factors but by my poor decision to be diligent. I allowed myself 99 days of freedom and 1 day of discipline. Then I became frustrated with external factors when I struggled to manage disruptions and emergencies on the day I became motivated to get some work done. I should have approached my earlier educational days with the mindset of having 99 workdays and 1 free day, as this would have built up my confidence and self-esteem and allowed me to enjoy the breaks that naturally happen. When asked to do something with others or when an emergency arose, it would be a nice break in my diligence rather than a hindrance.

Critical Thinking and Culture

The world is a complex blend of cultures, each offering its perspective. Every person uniquely represents their culture, and societies are the collective expressions of many individuals. To overlook the complexity and interconnectedness of these cultures is to trap oneself in the confines of narrow-mindedness. Therefore, it's important to remember that choosing to hold such views is ultimately our decision. We have the power to view cultures as complex or simplistic as we choose.

When humanity engages in open dialogue about culture, expressing how its complexities intertwine with society, the confinement of close-mindedness dissolves. Acknowledging the intricate nature of cultures leads to freedom from 'mentally imprisoned' and paves the way to openly express cultural identities. Having the philosophy of openly discussing complex topics and of hearing and acknowledging other points of view on complex cultural issues does not imprison anyone but frees them.

When considering culture, one often thinks of the rich tapestry of foods, languages, celebrations, music, and clothing in different parts of the world. These elements are just a few examples of the components that contribute to the beauty and diversity of cultures. Generally speaking, cultures are an umbrella term that encompasses social behaviors, institutions, and societal norms. These areas, among many others, shape how individuals interact with one another and influence collective values and practices within a community. Moreover, culture is not static; it evolves through the influence of historical events, technological advancements, and cross-cultural exchanges, reflecting the complexities and diversities inherent within human societies.

The term 'culture' encompasses the knowledge and beliefs of individuals that shape a community's identity. It includes many things, such as humanitarian arts, the laws upheld, and the customs and habits practiced. These cultural complexities provide a dynamic environment for culture to grow. Therefore, diversity should not be a source of conflict when understanding cultures but a cause for appreciation and admiration, highlighting the beauty of human creativity and adaptability.

People acquire cultural ideals through learning. You can be a child growing up in a culture or someone looking into a culture from the outside; the process is the same: it is learned. What is understood is that cultural norms govern society's conduct and serve as guidelines for cultural attributes such as behavior, dress, language, and personal characteristics. The guidelines serve as a template for normal expectations, setting boundaries that divide cultures and allow one to distinguish between them.

Norms encompass cultural universals such as music, dance, art style, religion, cooking, shelter, and clothing. These norms are the surface of cultures; they are culture's materials and physical dimensions. They are readily seen and experienced at any distance. In contrast, immaterial expressions of culture include principles such as social organizations (political), philosophy (written and verbal), and the intangibles of culture, such as heritage. They are not readily seen or experienced at any distance but instead on closer examination.

Given the complexities of cultural interpretation, it's essential to reflect on our own experiences and values, as well as those of others, to avoid potential cultural conflicts. For instance, a person from a culture that values direct communication might find the indirect communication style of another culture confusing or even disrespectful. However, to avoid potential conflicts caused by cultural differences and to remain open to other cultures, a person must critically evaluate their own experiences and the cultural values of others. Thinking critically about cultures helps a person avoid stereotypical tendencies. Critically examining one's own culture, as well as one's understanding of it, can help shape our insights into the meaning of another culture.

When a person finds joy in music in one culture, it is reasonable to assume that music is a source of pleasure in another culture, even if both styles of music are different in melody, tempo, and rhythm. Critical thinking skills empower individuals to bridge cultural gaps and recognize that differences are not grounds for judgment but opportunities for a richer understanding that can build bridges between them. This approach to critical thinking helps navigate differences and resolve cultural misunderstandings more effectively and empowers individuals to appreciate and respect cultural diversity.

Critical thinking enables individuals to navigate their own lives and understand others' experiences by interpreting and perceiving various situations. Cultural materialism in the social sciences posits that human symbolic culture arises from the conditions of human life. Symbolic culture refers to the capacity to inherit and transmit behaviors from one generation to the next. Furthermore, this transmission is achieved through the creation of symbols.

These symbols, such as anchors (representing hope and stability), balloons (representing childhood and freedom), bells (representing a warning or a wedding), and water (representing birth and life), carry cultural meanings and are used to pass down cultural values and beliefs. For example, a wedding ring is a symbolic object that represents love and commitment in many cultures. Thus, there are not only cultural differences, but also symbols that cross over many cultures. There are tens of thousands, if not more, common symbols from A to Z that identify cultures, the individuals within them, and connections among them. Thinking critically about the symbols used in one's culture helps one better understand other cultures.

Since cultural relativism holds that cultures cannot be objectively ranked, it follows that judging another culture's beliefs or practices based on one's own cultural standards is wrong. Therefore, it is crucial to recognize and appreciate cultural diversity and avoid making judgments about it. This mindset, developed through critical reflection on your culture, opens the door to a world of understanding and acceptance. Critical thinking is a tool for recognizing the positive attributes of comparative attributes.

What is your definition of *culture*? Write it down so you can revisit and reflect on it.

How is *culture* tied to critical thinking?

How has your idea of *culture* (or lack of) impacted your life up to this point?

How do critical thinking skills strengthen a person's sense of *culture*?

Explain how developing a progressive sense of *culture* can positively impact a person's life.

Explain how the absence of developing a sense of *culture* may hurt a person's life. (For instance, avoiding potential dangers, understanding personal emotions, etc.)

Express how you feel about *culture* being one of the most essential things in a successful life. (You may need to define the term successful.)

About the Author

Douglas Allan Portello lives in Washington State and is known for his strong ties to the local community and his commitment to helping others. Since 2013, he has worked as an educator, encouraging young adults to grow through self-reflection. He shares these ideas in his book series, *Freedom of Choice, No Freedom of Consequences.* The four books use real-life stories to teach lessons that young adults can relate to and use in their own lives. This helps them better understand the impact of their choices.

Outside of work, he enjoys spending time outdoors and values being with friends and family. He believes in lifelong learning and keeps growing by staying involved with the changing world. He has earned several master's degrees, including two in psychology and sociology, as well as a doctorate in education. He believes that earned education, gathered knowledge, and experiences are something we should share, as they are extremely valuable to those who possess them and to those who receive them.

Made in the USA
Coppell, TX
12 June 2026

81439447R00154